Qualitative Methods
in Sociolinguistics

Qualitative Methods
in
Sociolinguistics

Barbara Johnstone
Carnegie Mellon University

New York   Oxford
Oxford University Press
2000

Oxford University Press

Oxford   New York
Athens   Auckland   Bangkok   Bogotá   Buenos Aires   Calcutta
Cape Town   Chennai   Dar es Salaam   Delhi   Florence   Hong Kong   Istanbul
Karachi   Kuala Lumpur   Madrid   Melbourne   Mexico City   Mumbai
Nairobi   Paris   São Paulo   Singapore   Taipei   Tokyo   Toronto   Warsaw

and associated companies in
Berlin   Ibadan

Published by Oxford University Press, Inc.,
198 Madison Avenue, New York, New York 10016
http://www.oup-usa.org

Oxford is a registered trademark of Oxford University Press

Library of Congress Cataloging-in-Publication Data
Johnstone, Barbara.
    Qualitative methods in sociolinguistics / Barbara
Johnstone.
       p.   cm.
    Includes bibliographical references and index.
    ISBN 0-19-513397-8 (paper : alk. paper)
    1. Sociolinguistics—Research—Methodology.   I. Title.
P40.3.J64   2000
306.44'07'2—dc21   99-33400
                                                        CIP

Printing (last digit): 9 8 7 6 5 4 3 2
Printed in the United States of America
on acid-free paper

Contents

101451

Preface

This book is meant for people who want to do sociolinguistic research, be they undergraduates or graduate students taking a course in sociolinguistics, dissertation writers, professors changing subfields, or people who are just curious about the field. It is an overview of qualitative research techniques, not an overview of the field as a whole. In an introductory course about sociolinguistics, this book could complement materials about sociolinguistic theory and research findings. It could also be the text, or one of the texts, for a field methods course for students who have already been introduced to sociolinguistics. Because relatively few working sociolinguists were explicitly trained in research methodology, and because more sociolinguistics students have backgrounds in the humanities than in the sciences, the book begins with basic questions such as these: What does "empirical" mean? Is sociolinguistics a science? Is there a role for hypothesis-testing in interpretive, humanistic scholarship? What standards of evidence can we agree on?

Chapter 1 introduces the book's major themes. To contextualize what sociolinguists do, Chapter 2 sketches the field methods and/or analytical methods of three branches of linguistics that have in one way or another been precursors to contemporary sociolinguistics: dialect geography, which provides an interesting example of the interplay between preplanned rigor and spontaneous creativity in fieldwork; descriptive linguistics, which involves both well-articulated field methods such as elicitation techniques and well-articulated "discovery procedures" for the analysis of the collected corpus, and historical/comparative linguistics, in which field research (epigraphy, decipherment, textual criticism) is typically left to others and the emphasis is on rigorous methods of analysis—underpinned, as are all analytical methodologies, by leaps of intuition. Chapter 3 poses questions about methodology in general. What are data? What does it mean to do empirical work? What is a research question? How do qualitative and quantitative approaches complement each other? To people who are already engaged in sociolinguistic research, the answers to some of these questions will seem obvious. To beginners, the answers are often not obvious, and the questions can be intimidating, some particularly to humanists and others particularly to scientists. In Chapter 4 I raise some legal and ethical issues that necessitate thought and planning before any sort of research is undertaken. These include informed consent, funding, and the use of students as fieldworkers; the roles in scholarship of ideology, power, and politics; and the fuzzy boundary between "descriptive" and "critical" work. Chapter 5 deals with standards of evidence. Are there counterparts to scientific "validity" and "reliability" in qualitative work? How is the researcher likely to affect the research situation and subjects?

Each of the following three chapters treats one general way of working in qualitative sociolinguistics: intuition and introspection (Chapter 6), which are often the basis of good research ideas; observing, and in particular participant observation (Chapter 7); and reading and listening as practiced by discourse analysts (Chapter 8). In each chapter I consider both field methods and analytical methods, and in each chapter I illustrate the approach in question by describing studies that have employed it. Some of the illustrations involve work that is famous in the field, and some are descriptions of students' beginning work. The book's final chapter is about writing, with a section about the formats sociolinguists use and a section about how to write so as to avoid overgeneralization. If the book were being used as a text, this chapter could profitably be assigned toward the end of the course, when students were writing up projects or research proposals.

To make the book useful as the main text for a methods course or a supplementary text in a more general sociolinguistics course, I provide ideas for discussion in connection with each chapter except the first. These could be the basis for weekly assignments (though some of them, such as transcription practice, are quite time consuming); some could be the basis for larger studies to be carried out over the course of a semester.

I did not set out to write this book because I was an expert on methodology. In fact, research methodology has always been a source of insecurity for me, as I suspect it is for many sociolinguists. My claim to having anything at all to say is based on the fact that I have done a variety of different kinds of work and that some of it has involved trying out some new ways of collecting and analyzing data. (I will mention some of these when they are relevant.) Having written the book, I am still not an expert on methodology, but simply a working sociolinguist who has given the matter some systematic thought. I hope it will be useful to other professionals as well as to newcomers.

Mary Bucholtz at Texas A&M University, Heidi Ehernberger Hamilton at Georgetown University, and Susan Berk-Seligson and Christina Bratt Paulston at the University of Pittsburgh have tested parts or all of a draft of this book in their classes. I am grateful to them and to their students for their feedback. Bucholtz and Hamilton provided particularly detailed and valuable critiques. I am also grateful to the members of two graduate sociolinguistics discussion groups at Carnegie Mellon University, who read the whole manuscript with rhetorical and critical eyes and gave me many useful suggestions. The groups' members were Martha Cheng, Dan Dewey, Rocio Dominguez, Ann McAuliffe, Frank McKeown, Atreyee Phukan, Christina Stile, Susan Swan, Laura Tomokiyo, Yukiko Wada, Amanda Young, Danielle Zawodny-Wetzel, and Sean Zdenek. Thanks also to William Kretzschmar for originally suggesting that I take on this project, and to all the colleagues, coauthors, research assistants, and anonymous reviewers who have, over the years, tried to keep me honest and explicit about my own research methods.

◆ 1 ◆

Introduction

Sociolinguists are people with training in linguistics and a primary interest in questions about what language is like, how it works, and what its functions are. Sociolinguists make and defend claims about how language use is both constrained and enabled by, for example, the social and rhetorical context of an utterance (who says it, to whom, where and when, for what purpose, and so on), the medium in which a message is transmitted, and the linguistic context (what came before and what comes afterward). Many sociolinguists focus on variation—why not everyone talks alike—and the relationship between linguistic variation and language change. Some are particularly interested in how ways of talking function as claims to and displays of people's social class, gender, ethnicity, and social and personal identity. Others are interested in the details of conversations and monologues, in how speakers manage to create turns to talk, topics, speech actions such as orders and requests, and structural subparts such as introductions, middles, and conclusions.

Whatever its focus, sociolinguistic work is based on observations of people using language and analyses of those observations. Unlike, say, philosophical claims, sociolinguistic claims do not result entirely from mental speculation or arise in discussions among sociolinguists strolling in the agora. To ensure that they are observing what they think they are observing and that they are seeing or hearing a sample of it that is adequate and representative, sociolinguists have methods for collecting their data in a systematic way, whether the data consist of speech or signing or writing, by one person or many, on one topic or several. To ensure that they

1

are describing the data completely and fairly and interpreting it conscientiously, sociolinguists have analytical methods, either strictly defined procedures for coding and counting, looser lists of things to take into account, or general strategies for reading or listening.

From the beginning, sociolinguists have engaged in qualitative as well as quantitative research. Since Dell Hymes (1974) and John J. Gumperz (1982; Gumperz and Hymes, 1972) first suggested ethnography and interpretive close reading as ways of studying language use as it affects and is affected by social and cultural context, interest in qualitative approaches to the study of language in use has expanded rapidly. There are now thousands of people who work in this paradigm, typically calling what they do "ethnography of communication," "interactional sociolinguistics," or "discourse analysis." The findings of qualitative sociolinguists are by now consistently mentioned in textbooks. Texts by Fasold (1984, 1990), Hudson (1996), and Wardhaugh (1997), for example, discuss work by scholars such as Bauman, Gumperz, Hymes, LePage and Tabouret-Keller, Ochs, Schiffrin, Sherzer, and Tannen. But the research methodology of these and the many other sociolinguists whose work is based primarily on close observation, reading, and listening is typically discussed only in passing.

This has to do with the fact that sociolinguists do not usually talk about methodology much except when they are describing their own projects. Books and articles about specific sociolinguistic studies usually outline the data-collection methods that were used, telling how the investigator decided what to observe and how it was observed. Often, though less consistently, sociolinguists discuss their analytical methods, either in detail ("Calculations A, B, and C were performed, and the results subjected to statistical tests X, Y, and Z") or more sketchily ("We looked for examples of D and E"). Oddly, though, there have been no treatments of sociolinguistic methodology in general, except in the area of quantitative variation studies as carried out by Labov (1984) and Milroy (1987a). There are books about nonquantitative, interpretive research methods in education, communication studies, sociology, and anthropology, many of which I will draw on and recommend in what follows, but none about qualitative research in sociolinguistics.

But there are reasons for all sociolinguists to think about research methodology more carefully than we have in the past. For one thing, because we are asking more questions and different questions than we previously did, we need more ways of answering them. We are turning from an examination of relatively homogeneous societies to more heterogeneous ones. The list of variables we consider, which included biological characteristics such as age and sex and attributed ones such as gender and ethnicity, has been expanded to include things about people that are harder to see, such as social identification, tastes, and preferences as well as individual identity. With new technologies for storing and processing information, sources of data multiply and data sets grow. In Europe, where "pragmatics" means approximately what "sociolinguistics" does in North America, the *Handbook of Pragmatics* (Verschueren et al. 1995) lists 16 primary methods, from "contrastive analysis" through "error analysis, ethnography, experimentation" to "taxonomy." This volume will taxonomize somewhat less, classifying methods into larger groups, but it is intended to help people whose reading in sociolinguistics has been mainly centered on research *topics* (therapeutic discourse, or individual variation, or code switching in Malaysia) to see what the range of qualitative methodologies can be.

Another reason for thinking about methodology is the general atmosphere of skepticism in the humanities and social sciences. Postmodern critical theory suggests that, at the least, we ought to examine our assumptions about how objective observation can be and whether interpretation can arrive at truth. Literary scholars, historians, anthropologists, and sociologists wonder to what extent evidence is "socially constructed," the result of shared biases rather than an objective sign of fact. Seeing science, history, and criticism as results of discursive practices (ways of talking and thinking) handed down and enforced by dominant social groups, they examine how standards of evidence and modes of proof are historically situated. (See, for example, Chandler et al., 1994.) At its most frightening (or most liberating), critical theory claims that observations and observers are hopelessly intertwined, and that any text can mean anything. Debate over such ideas has enlivened discourse in anthropology and other humanistic and social scientific disciplines, but it has barely touched sociolinguistics. This book will not be and will not include an overview of postmodernism or of the philosophy of science in general, but it is meant, in part, to encourage sociolinguists to think about where they stand on issues of objectivity and truth.

Four phases of research methodology will be treated in the chapters that follow:

- *Developing Research Questions*. As we will see, much sociolinguistic research begins when sociolinguists find themselves in sites or situations that seem as if they might be interesting to study. With only the rarest exceptions, sociolinguists do not first decide what hypotheses to test and then seek out the ideal sources of data; rich and interesting language use is everywhere, and we take advantage of this fact. Having identified something that might be of interest for sociolinguistic study, the first step is to decide precisely what is potentially interesting about it. This involves articulating half-formed hunches into clear, answerable questions. I will offer some suggestions about how to formulate research questions and illustrate how sociolinguists actually did so in several cases.

- *Field Methods*. How do sociolinguists assemble the material for qualitative analyses? This depends on the kind of work they are doing: sometimes it involves observing, sometimes listening, sometimes reading, sometimes asking people to do things. Often it begins with introspection. I will describe and illustrate each of these methodologies and some of the specific steps they involve, such as tape-recording and transcribing, interviewing, and learning systematic ways of listening to people's talk and watching them do things with language.

- *Analytical Methods*. How are the data analyzed? Again, there are various approaches, and we will consider several. We will look at analytical heuristics for qualitative study, lists, that is, of questions to ask about the data to ensure that nothing has been left out. We will talk about classifying, perhaps the most basic way of making sense of piles of information bits. We will also discuss the uses—and abuses—of counting and calculating in research that is primarily not quantitative.

- *Writing*. How is sociolinguistic research written up? There are various ways: some write essays whereas others write articles modeled more on scientific genres. I will illustrate both. I will also discuss what I call "the grammar of particularity." Our work is almost always very particular: we describe the particular texts, people, or communities we study. We expect readers to make some tentative generalizations based on those particularities, asking themselves whether what we found might be true elsewhere, too, but we also have to avoid overgeneralizing: making claims about "women" based on the behavior of a few Midwesterners or claims about directions of language change based on the behavior of a few college students. There are several syntactic choices we can discipline ourselves to make that minimize this risk somewhat: ways to describe things that keep reminding readers that the descriptions are particular, and ways to talk about numbers that do not rhetorically inflate them.

Summary

Sociolinguists have always used qualitative as well as quantitative research methods, but we have rarely discussed our qualitative methods explicitly. It is important that we do so because we are asking some different questions than we once did and using more kinds of data, and because increased reflexivity about research in the humanities and social sciences requires us to justify what we do more carefully than was once thought necessary. In this book, we discuss several phases of research: the development of research questions, field methods, qualitative methods of analysis (in particular, ethnography and discourse analysis), and writing up the results of qualitative studies.

Suggestions for Further Reading

Overviews of sociolinguistics include Hudson (1996), Fasold (1984, 1990), and Wardhaugh (1997). General guides to qualitative research are Denzin and Lincoln (1994), Lindlof (1995; with an emphasis on communication), and Alasuutari (1995; with an emphasis on cultural studies).

◆ 2 ◆

Methodology in Historical Context

Contemporary sociolinguistics has its roots in several branches of linguistics as well as in anthropology and sociology. Sociolinguists whose research questions are about language change carry on the tradition of historical/comparative linguists. Those interested in social and regional variation often use data collected by dialectologists, in a field-method tradition initiated in the nineteenth century. Ethnographers of communication, who study ways of speaking in their cultural contexts, draw on research techniques developed in anthropology and descriptive linguistics. Turn-by-turn sociolinguistic analyses of conversations borrow from the methodology of Conversation Analysis developed by sociologists.

To provide some historical context for the discussion in the chapters to follow and to illustrate the interplay between field methods and analytical methods, this chapter discusses methodology in three of the precursors to sociolinguistics: dialectology, structuralist descriptive linguistics, and historical/comparative linguistics. It is not intended to be a complete exposition or critique of any of these fields, but rather to say just enough to illustrate some of the variety in the sources of our research techniques.

Field Methods in American Dialect Geography

The North American dialect atlas project was originally conceived as a Linguistic Atlas of the United States and Canada. Plans for the project began in the late 1920s, when the American Council of

6

Learned Societies, which funded the first data-collection phases, appointed a planning committee. Because of its relatively small size, New England was chosen as the first research site, and fieldwork was carried out there between 1931 and 1933. *The Linguistic Atlas of New England* (LANE) was thus the first to be completed (see Kurath et al., 1939–1943); later surveys were *The Linguistic Atlas of the Upper Midwest* (LAUM; see Allen, 1973–1976), *The Linguistic Atlas of the North Central States* (LANCS; see McDavid, 1976–1978), *The Linguistic Atlas of the Gulf States* (LAGS; see Pederson et al., 1986–1992), and *The Linguistic Atlas of the Middle and South Atlantic States* (LAMSAS; see Kretzschmar et al., 1993). A related project was DARE, the *Dictionary of American Regional English* (Cassidy 1985, 1991, 1996), for which surveys were conducted nationwide. Because of the expense of the research, and because social and geographic mobility has made it increasingly difficult to identify regional speech forms, the Dialect Atlas of the United States and Canada has never been finished, although the maps, worksheets, recordings, and electronic databases that resulted from the completed surveys are still in use.

Field methods for the dialect atlas projects were relatively well elaborated: planned in advance, spelled out in detail, and consistent from researcher to researcher and project to project. Field methods for the American studies were borrowed from the large European dialect geography projects, especially those of Gilliéron in France and Jaberg and Jud in Italy and southern Switzerland. Fieldworkers were trained in descriptive linguistics, particularly in phonetics; because tape recording was not feasible in the early days, transcriptions were made on the spot, by the fieldworkers themselves.

Fieldworkers assigned to an area selected their informants, trying to find people who had been born in the area and had lived there almost uninterruptedly. Because the atlas projects had ultimately arisen in the attempt to collect folk speech in Europe, the preference was for the oldest rural settlements, although cities were also included. Informants were classified into three groups by their level of education, how much they read, and how much contact they had with people from elsewhere. (These groups usually also corresponded with age groups, as the oldest informants would be the least "cultured" and have the least education.) Attempts were made to find about an equal number of women and men.

The atlas fieldworkers' task was to elicit around 800 items from each informant, most focusing on pronunciation and lexicon, fewer on such morphological matters as the preterit and participial forms of irregular verbs. They were provided with a worksheet describing the items they were to collect; it was up to them to decide how to elicit them. (The exception was the DARE project, for which field-workers had to use the exact wording of the questionnaire and not suggest responses except as a last-ditch measure.) The items were for the most part everyday concepts related to work, nature, and social life. Fieldworkers usually used indirect questions, holding up or pointing to something and asking "What do you call this?," devising a fill-in-the blank, or describing a situation and asking for a term for it, rather than asking direct questions such as "What do you call a firefly?" or "What do you call a cup?" Sometimes, after receiving a different initial response, fieldworkers would suggest the word they had in mind. Questions were usually organized in semantic groups, so that respondents would get involved in conversations on topics such as farming, kinship, or the weather. Transcripts of parts of one LAGS interview (Pederson, 1974) show that the interviews were often fairly open-ended, relaxed conversations, especially when conducted by talented, experienced fieldworkers. DARE interviews regularly included the informant's tape-recorded reading aloud of a story designed to capture a variety of phonetic and phonological features, and half an hour of taped talk on any subject. As they recorded responses in narrow phonetic transcription, fieldworkers also made notes about other things the informants said that related to the questionnaire items, such as whether a word was old-fashioned, new, or one the informant had heard but did not use. Complete interviews were long, often lasting more than 8 hours, depending on the informant's personality and the interviewer's skill at creating rapport.

The primary results of the earlier dialect atlas projects were actual atlases: collections of maps. The atlas that resulted from the New England survey, for example, consisted of a map for each item that was elicited, with transcriptions of its varying pronunciations inked next to the fieldwork sites where they were collected. Later surveys have made information available in a larger variety of ways, such as in computer databases [see, for example, Kretzschmar et al. (1993) for LAMSAS and Pederson (1993) for LAGS]. Attempts were made to collect the same information everywhere and transcribe it the

---

Box 2.1 Excerpt From an Interview for *The Linguistic Atlas of the Gulf States*

This excerpt is from an interview with a 76-year-old farmer from Sevier County, Tennessee (Pederson, 1974, pp. 20–21).

INTERVIEWER: Yesterday when we were taking about hogs, I forgot to ask you what you call a hog that's been fixed or castrated.

INFORMANT: Barry. [barrow]

INTERVIEWER: Would you say that again please.

INFORMANT: Barry. I don't know how that's spelled, b-a-r-r-y I guess. He's a boar till he's trimmed, I mean, and you'd call it caster-rated. Anyway, it takes his seed out. Then he's a barry. Well, that's the kind you fatten. You can't eat boar meat. I don't know how they do it. I've been to the stock-yards and see them fellers buy 'em by truckloads, but I don't know how they do it. You kill a boar, and you can't eat it. Or you kill a sow that's in season, you know—a'boarin'— you can't eat that. Used to, when we killed sows, we had to watch that awfully close. You get one in there. You can't eat it. They're just strong. You can smell it!

Fella up here 'bove me, I used to take my sows up there. He had a great big boar. I guess he'd weigh six or seven hundred pounds. He's mean! And they got to they couldn't do nothin' with him and this here fella let his renter have the boar. He had a big family. And he let him have that, and they kill it, and they couldn't eat it. . . .

---

same way, but because of inevitable differences among fieldworkers in interviewing style, selection of informants, and habits of transcription, "anyone attempting to use [a dialect atlas] for interpretive purposes must carefully study all the information available about its structure and collection and be on the alert for contrasts and variables that may be artifacts of the way these matters are handled and presented" (Francis, 1993, p. 15). In the words of the coordinator of the LAGS project, "a linguistic atlas works best in the hands of a craftsman" (Pederson, 1993, p. 33).

What *have* craftspeople done with this rich body of information? In addressing this question, we turn from methods for collecting data to methods for analyzing it. Whereas field methods in dialect geography are relatively elaborated, analytical methods are not. Dialect atlas surveys were not usually carried out with very specific research questions in mind, and people have done various things with the resulting data, and in various ways, depending on the questions they ask. Some approaches are quantitative, involving arguments based on counting items of various kinds; other are qualitative, based instead or in addition on looking at the data in other ways.

One of the tasks of dialectologists is to identify and explain the boundaries of dialect areas. There are at least two ways of using dialect atlas material to do this. One is to use maps, drawing "isoglosses," or lines that separate the areas in which different forms are used. Bundles of coinciding isoglosses mark dialect boundaries, which often coincide with geographic boundaries such as rivers or mountain ranges, or with social boundaries such as political borders. Historical settlement patterns can be traced in patterns of dialect difference. Another way of studying boundaries is to count the numbers of times given forms are used in given areas. Chambers and Trudgill's (1980) *Dialectology* gives many examples of studies of both kinds.

Other dialectologists focus on the reasons for dialect differences, making less use of maps and more use of the demographic information that was collected from each informant. Researchers ask whether differences in word choice are correlated with gender, for example, or with level of education, and how those correlations intersect with regional differences. (One example is Johnson, 1996.) Information collected for dialect atlases has been used in other ways as well (see, for example, the studies in Allen and Underwood, 1971).

Field Methods and "Discovery Procedures" in Descriptive Linguistics

The designers of the dialect atlas projects were explicit about field methods but not about analytical methods. Their field research resulted in large, rich bodies of carefully collected data that they and others could then use to answer various questions. Descriptive linguists in the American tradition of Bloomfield (1933, 1942), on the other hand, were explicit about both field methods and analytical methods. This had in part to do with the tenor of the times: linguistics was seen as "the science of language," and absolute rigor in method of inquiry was thought to result in absolute truth. It also had to do with the fact that, in theory, descriptive linguists were all asking the same question: "What is the structure of language x?" Still (though this was not usually overtly acknowledged at first), field methods in descriptive linguistics have often been learned largely by watching others or through trial and error, and (as in any science) analysis often involves intuitive leaps.

Though Bloomfield said nothing about field methods in his textbook, *Language* (1933), and methods of analysis have to be inferred from his descriptions of linguistic structure, he paid specific attention to field research in a brochure published by the Linguistic Society of America in 1942, *Outline Guide for the Practical Study of Foreign Languages*. The technique has changed little since then, except that tape recording has made the job easier in some ways and harder in others. Since Chomskyan generative approaches have in large part supplanted structuralist approaches to phonology, syntax, and other aspects of linguistic structure, and because there are fewer and fewer undescribed languages left, field methods and structuralist analytical methods are less and less frequently taught. [Newman (1992) reports on a survey of 42 U.S. linguistics departments, only 28 of which regularly offered a field methods course. At one time such a course was a requirement in any American Ph.D. program in linguistics.] But there are several books that describe the techniques, for readers who are interested in exploring it further. (See the suggestions at the end of this chapter.)

The core field technique in descriptive linguistics is "elicitation," the collection and transcription of short utterances that illustrate linguistic features relevant to an analysis of some part of the linguistic system. In contrast with the dialect atlas researchers, fieldworkers in the descriptive linguistics tradition are the primary users of the data they collect. Their data collection is thus keyed to their own ongoing analysis of the language they are studying. Fieldworkers beginning with no knowledge of the language have to rely at first on assumptions about what they will find, based on descriptions of related languages and on what is known about language universals. (For example, the language will almost certainly have nouns and verbs, although not all words will be in the same class as they are in English.) For some language families there are word lists and guides developed by others for "scheduled" elicitation. [Bouquiaux and Thomas (1992) contains a set of these designed for use in west Africa, for example.] "Analytical" elicitation is designed on the spot to assemble data meant to answer specific questions. The researcher might, for example, wonder which part of a previously elicited utterance meant what, and try to find out by presenting the informant with systematic permutations of the meaning of the utterance to translate or by requesting the informant to substitute one word for another or correct the researcher's version of a sentence. Elicited utterances are initially transcribed in narrow phonetic detail using

---

Box 2.2   Scheduled Elicitation:
Excerpt From a Thematic Questionnaire

This questionnaire was designed for fieldworkers in Africa. It is adapted from Cloarec-Heiss (1992). This part of the much longer verb questionnaire elicits contrasts having to do with person, number, and grammatical gender in clauses that describe continuous action in the present.

1. Present

1.1	I	is walking/
1.2	you (SG)	is not walking
1.3	he/she/it	
1.4	we (including you SG/you PL)	
1.5	we (excluding you SG/you PL)	
1.6	we two	is making/
1.7	you two	is not making
1.8	you (PL)	
1.9	they (M) / they (F) / they (neuter)	
1.10	they two (M) / they two (F) / they two (neuter)	
1.11	What are you doing? I am crushing the grain.	
1.12	He is coming to ask for a pestle.	

the International Phonetic Alphabet (IPA) or a similar system. Once the language's phonemic system begins to become clear, broader transcription is used.

Elicitation is not without its pitfalls. The researcher may be asking for a name ("Amazon"), for example, and getting a description ("a big river") or asking for a specific term (such as the name of a particular species of plant) and getting a generic one ("plant"); all sorts of variation are of course possible as a function of factors such as formality. People may not want researchers to write down forms they think of as incorrect, for example. Bilingual translators can introduce complication, and in monolingual settings where there is no interpreter, informants may adopt a kind of "foreigner talk" for communicating with the researchers, simplifying their syntax and limiting their lexical choices. If work is done with more than one informant at a time, there may be competition among them. For these reasons, among others, it is important to work with the right people. As we will see later on, this is a more complex issue than most descriptivists acknowledged, but thought was given to the matter and it is treated in the manuals I mentioned above. Other practical matters are dealt with as well: how to tape-record and the limitations of tape-recording (it is easy to collect more data than can ever be transcribed), how to make notes and organize them, how to listen most productively in the earliest phases (by focusing on one sound at a time), and how to make sessions with informants go smoothly and productively (by taking regular breaks, for example).

Fieldwork in descriptive linguistics is in general more improvisatory than fieldwork for dialectology, partly because research sites and situations vary so much. What constituted enough data for the dialect atlas workers was defined in advance: the 800 items on their worksheets. What constitutes enough data for the description of a language is far harder to define, and descriptive linguists have always found themselves moving back and forth between data collection and analysis. In addition to elicitation, fieldworkers also collected longer texts such as myths and other stories, and, once tape recorders became available, they taped whole speech events. This material could also serve as data.

Analytical methods in structuralist linguistics are often called "discovery procedures." These are in essence the procedures intro-ductory linguistics students learn to solve problems in phonology, morphology, and syntax. The difference, of course, is that field researchers do not start with preselected sets of relevant data, but rather with hundreds or thousands of transcribed elicitations. Structuralist linguists, unlike generativists, were not willing to posit structures in the mind predisposing humans to come to certain kinds of conclusions about languages and not others; how a form worked was thought to be deduced entirely on the basis of what it could replace (its paradigmatic relations) and what it could cooccur with (its syntagmatic relations). This meant that there had to be a rigorously stated set of mechanical procedures for starting with physical data (in the form of a narrowly transcribed corpus of speech) and arriving at an analysis—since this was, after all, what native speakers were thought to do as they learned their own languages. The central technique is to identify contrasts in meaning correlated with contrasts in sound or structure. This means finding minimal pairs, sets of utterances that differ in only one way and mean different things. (The levels at which this system worked best were phonology and morphology; structuralists described syntax in somewhat looser ways.) The results were a list of the phonemes of the language and a set of statements about relations among them (which could precede or follow others, for example), and a list of the morphemes and their interrelations.

As even the most science-minded descriptivists acknowledged, these discovery procedures were never actually as mechanical as might have been hoped. Even the first step, segmenting a stream of sound into transcribable units, requires some prior knowledge of what the relevant segments are likely to be. Bloomfield wrote that "the analysis and recording of languages will remain an art or a practical skill" (1933, p. 93) as long as "science" cannot analyze meaning in any mechanical way, and this skill is learned more easily if the analyst knows something about what differences are likely to be distinctive in various language types. Intuitions based on experience and knowledge about likely possibilities are often the basis for guesses that become hypotheses to be tested. (Anyone who has taken or taught introductory linguistics has noticed this. The simplest phonology problem can be a complete mystery to someone who does not know that consonant voicing or vowel height may be a relevant fact.) For this reason, descriptive methodology is taught more by example than from books. The typical "field methods" course is a semester or two of work with an informant hired by the professor. With the professor's guidance, students take turns eliciting data from the informant, and at the end of the term they hand in their phonological and morphological analyses of the language. Demonstrations of elicitation techniques by experienced researchers are another fairly common teaching technique.

Analytical Methods in Historical/ Comparative Linguistics

Unlike descriptive linguistics or dialectology, traditional historical/comparative linguistics has no field methods. (Contemporary sociolinguistic work on language change, on the other hand, relies heavily on fieldwork, much of it based on methods pioneered by William Labov, which will be discussed later.) This is to say that, unlike descriptivists or dialectologists, traditional historical linguists do not create their data sets through survey or elicitation. Instead, they work with data discovered and recorded by others; they may take an interest in the sources of the material they work with, but for the most part they would not have been qualified to produce the material themselves, not being archaeologists, epigraphers, or philologists.

Like descriptive linguistics, however, historical/comparative linguistics has an analytical methodology that is at least in theory fairly rigorous. This is called "the comparative method" and it involves two kinds of "reconstruction," internal and external. This is not the place to explain the procedures in detail. Briefly, external reconstruction involves laying out cognate words in a range of related languages and arriving at a linguistic common denominator, a hypothetical protoform that could have given rise to them all. Internal reconstruction means comparing forms within a language over time and hypothesizing still earlier forms on the basis of the trajectory of change.

As with descriptive analytical methodology, it is helpful to know what sorts of patterns are likely; the comparative method, like the descriptivists' "discovery procedures," relies on intuitions based on previous knowledge. Hence courses in historical linguistics focus much attention on what phonological, morphological, phonetic, lexical, and syntactic change tends to be like (for example, phonemes are more likely to coalesce than to split over time) and on issues such as the effects of language contact. Somewhat less attention is typically paid to the evidence on which comparativists' claims are based: the data and its collection. Historical/comparative linguists often work with written texts, but issues connected with the collection and evaluation of the texts are usually left to scholars in other fields. Such issues include, for example, the decipherment of unknown writing systems, the transmission of texts over time and the ways errors can be introduced in the process, and the provenance of texts and how likely they are to be good representations of the languages in which they are written.

General Themes

These three historical sketches highlight several themes to which we will return. One is that linguists have not always found it necessary to be rigorous or explicit about both field methods and analytical methods. Linguistics sometimes means the collection of linguistic data, sometimes the analysis of linguistic data, and sometimes both. In contemporary sociolinguistics, analysis of one kind or another is almost always expected, and we will assume in what follows that the projects readers are working on are not exclusively data-collection efforts. Data-collection methods in sociolinguistics range from the assembling of texts created by others (as in historical/comparative linguistics) to the researchers' creation of their own sets of data by asking questions or assigning linguistic tasks (as in dialectology and descriptive linguistics).

Another theme is that research always involves both planning and improvisation. No a priori description of field or analytical techniques will ever predict exactly what the process will be like, what adaptations will need to be made on the data-collection spot, or what intuitive leaps will prove fruitful in the analysis, and no after-the-fact report of a research project ever details exactly what it was like. Because different fieldworkers are gifted in different ways, there is never only one procedure that will work. There are many ways to get people to talk unselfconsciously, for example; sometimes a respectful listener will have better luck and sometimes a rapport-building talker will. This does not mean, though, that anything will work as data. Despite their flexibility about data-collection procedures, both dialectologists and descriptivists know what kinds of information they are after, and if they are successful they collect that information (and perhaps other rich data as well).

A third theme is that the best analyses are based on a thorough grounding in the field. Just as the phonemic analysis of a specific language is made easier with increased knowledge about phonological systems, a good sociolinguistic project is based on experience with sociolinguistic possibilities. Interesting examples of language use are everywhere; sociolinguistics students rarely have trouble finding something to study. Knowing what to say about it, what questions to ask, and how to answer them is the hard part.

DISCUSSION QUESTIONS

Since this is the first set of discussion questions, a note to students and teachers: Most of these ideas involve tasks that seem very simple. But each one is more complex than it seems—and this is precisely the point! The actual data collection or analysis is often less important than the thought and discussion about methodology that should precede it.

1. Develop a research method to determine what people call the following, and collect data from 5 or 10 informants (either all from one area or from a variety of areas):
   - a large, overstuffed sandwich (submarine/sub/hoagie/ po-boy/ . . .)
   - a carbonated drink (pop/soda/soda water/Coke/soft drink/ . . .)
   - a pan used for frying (frying pan/skillet/ . . .)
   - a divided, limited-access road (freeway/Interstate/highway/ turnpike/ . . .)
   - a bed covering filled with feathers (quilt/duvet/comforter/ hap/featherbed/ . . .)

As you decide how to collect your data, consider these issues:
   - How are you going to select your sample? Will it consist of the first 5 or 10 people you come across, or a sample chosen to represent the population as a whole? If you decide on a representative sample, what variables will you consider? Sex? Ethnicity? Age? Urban or rural background? What else? Why?
   - How are you going to find the informants you need, and how will you approach them? A cold call over the phone around dinnertime? Through a mutual friend? By placing an ad? What

are the advantages and disadvantages of these and other techniques? What would be the advantages and disadvantages of paying informants?

- How are you going to describe to potential informants what you are doing and why? Fellow students usually do not object to helping each other with class projects, but what if it weren't a class project, but an actual dialect atlas survey? Should you get informants' consent in writing? How are you going to introduce yourself, given the fact that (as you've probably noticed) people get linguistically self-conscious around linguists and English teachers?
- How will you elicit the words? By holding up the items? By asking other kinds of indirect questions? By suggesting possible words? If you are doing this as a class, how important is it for everyone to use exactly the same technique?
- How will you record the responses? In phonetic transcription? In regular orthography? Should you tape record the interviews? Videotape them? Would people answer differently if they were being taped?

2. Find someone who speaks a language you do not know, preferably one that is in a different language family than your own, and find out how to say "I have a pen" in that language. Unless you get completely stuck, *do not use any English* and ask your informant not to speak English. Do not try to come up with the entire structure of the language; just learn how to say the sentence. Then (you can use English to elicit this) learn to say "thank you" and say it. Some ideas and hints:

- You may be able to elicit *pen* by holding one up. How will you know that the word you are hearing means "pen" and not "writing utensil" or "cylindrical thing"?
- Is there a verb *have* in every language?
- Some languages (Thai, for example) have several forms meaning "I."
- In most (if not all) languages speakers make different choices depending on how self-conscious they are, to whom they are talking, what they are talking about, and so on.
- Is there any reason to suppose a man might say the sentence differently than a woman?
- Does your informant have a regionally or socially marked accent?

- Use the IPA to transcribe. You may need to use some special diacritics. Is the language you are hearing a tone language? Your initial transcriptions will have to be fairly narrow phonetic ones. What detail do you include? Can you leave any out?
- Imagine doing this sort of work for hours at a time. Would your informant get bored or resentful? What might be the consequences? How would you avoid this?
- What do you think of the word "informant" for the person with whom you are working? Are there alternatives you like better?

Suggestions for Further Reading

Sources of information about the history and methodology of the dialect atlas projects are Allen (1956), Atwood (1971), Cassidy (1993), Chambers and Trudgill (1980), Francis (1993), and Pederson (1993). Samarin (1976), Kibrik (1977), and Bouquiaux and Thomas (1992) concentrate on field methods in descriptive linguistics and Harris (1951) concentrates on analytical methods. One of the many good sources about the comparative method in historical linguistics is Jeffers and Lehiste (1979).

◆ 3 ◆

Thinking About Methodology

The goal of this chapter is to enable beginners to start thinking of themselves as field researchers and data analysts, to begin to suggest what research is, and to introduce some of the theoretical issues surrounding it. The chapter poses some very basic questions about sociolinguistic research and suggests ways of thinking about answers to these questions. Some of the questions may seem simplistic to some readers, especially those who have been involved in empirical research projects. Some of the answers may seem to border on the naive, especially to those readers who have studied the philosophy of science. I will not try to provide answers to questions about the nature of knowing, which could be argued indefinitely, but I will try to enable would-be sociolinguists to work with and around prevailing (and for the most part healthy) postmodern skepticism about observation and objectivity. The chapter also describes how sociolinguists develop research questions and discusses the difference between qualitative and quantitative work.

What Is Research?

The kind of research most of us learn to do first is based on work in the library (or, more and more, via electronic media). In high school and college writing classes, we learn to choose a topic, develop a thesis about it, and find scholarly or popular sources that suggest whether the thesis is credible or not. The result of the project is a "research paper."

Sociolinguistic research also involves finding and interpreting scholarly sources. As we will see later, a report about a research project always incorporates, in one way or another, a "review of the literature," which is to say a summary of others' research on the topic. But the work sociolinguists do almost never consists only of library work. Sociolinguists' claims are based primarily on field research. This means that instead of finding support for or disconfirmation of their theses in the work of previous scholars, sociolinguists find it through analyses of samples of language that they collect.

In one sense, sociolinguistic research is no different from the everyday process by which we come to conclusions about people and language. Everyday "research" can be carried out in conversations among friends, in which people share their observations about others' behavior. Such conversations sometimes even give rise to fairly well-articulated research questions. For example, a group of friends might chat about talking to their parents on the phone. One person might observe that although she has no trouble talking with her father face to face, he never says anything on the phone, whereas her mother seems to talk on the phone even more than she does in person. Others might chime in with similar stories. Some might object: "No, in my family it's the other way." As the topic finally peters out, someone might propose a question as a way of providing closure: "I wonder whether women always talk more on the phone?"

Conversational questions like this can turn into research questions. This one, in fact, has, in a study of women and the telephone by Lana Rakow (1992). Beginning with the idea that the telephone served functions in at least some women's lives that it did not serve in men's, Rakow developed an ethnographic study of telephone use in a Midwestern farming community that shows, among other things, that communicative labor is divided there, the men engaging mainly in face-to-face talk whereas the women are responsible for telephone talk. What differentiates Rakow's research from the conversational speculation it may have originally been based on is that Rakow's work was *systematic*. Rather than forming a conclusion based on the experiences of a few people she happened to be talking to, Rakow set out to answer a set of specific questions about the telephone and women's talk, using a set of methods (in her case, mainly ethnographic ones) she decided on in advance. The systematicity of Rakow's study is what makes it research rather than just casual observation, and most of this book is about ways of being systematic: deciding what you are going to do and how to do it in advance, then doing it that way and documenting what you find.

It should be noted that not all questions can be turned into research questions. Some questions cannot be answered through observation. ("Does God exist?" might be one such.) Others might turn out to be too difficult to be answered easily, perhaps because they involve terms that are too hard to define. And there are fads in sociolinguistics, as in every other discipline. For a while, people get interested in narrative, for example; later they talk about cultural ideologies about language and then about individuality. Students often find themselves asking the kinds of questions their teachers are asking, sometimes as a result of direct advice to do so (a teacher can be more helpful if she or he is working in the same area) and sometimes because students do not know what else to do. At a given time, some endeavors will count as research and some will not, and what counts has more than a little to do with who reviews grant proposals and how faculty tenure cases are evaluated. (See Cameron, 1992, pp. 122–127 for more about the politics of scholarly research in linguistics.) This situation may not be ideal, but it is probably inevitable, and it is worth keeping in mind when new research projects are being developed. Tackling a question nobody has considered before may be a way of revolutionizing the field, or it may be a way of marginalizing the researcher, and teachers may owe it to students to help them find out where they stand vis-à-vis other researchers and research projects.

What Are Data?

In Latin, "data" means "things given." (The word "data" was originally a count noun, the plural of "datum." It is now sometimes used as a mass noun, with singular agreement.) Data are the result of observation, consisting of the "given things" that researchers analyze. Though not all sociolinguists call the material they analyze "data"—some feel that doing so makes an implied claim to a sort of hard-science methodology with which they are uncomfortable— all work with the results of systematic observations, either about texts, people, or situations.

As we all know, observations are not always trustworthy. It is all too easy to think that a person is angry who is actually lonely, not to remember a scene in a movie or to remember one that was not in it, or to imagine you heard something in the middle of the night. Observations are influenced by feelings and expectations, by unconscious "theories," in other words, about what usually happens or what is about to happen. (Linguists have called these "frames"; see, for example, Tannen, 1979.) Because observations are "theory laden" in this way, many humanists and social scientists have come to mistrust the ideas (associated with the philosophy of science known as "positivism") that systematic observation can yield the truth about reality and that scientific claims are falsifiable. At its extreme, postmodern critical theory claims that there are no such things as "truth" or "reality" or ways of determining if claims are valid or not. Yet in scholarly life as in everyday life, people continue to act as if the world were more or less the same for them as for others and to feel responsible for the truth or falsity of what they say, and scholarly research (including the making and defense of claims in critical theory) continues.

Cameron et al. (1992, pp. 6–10) suggest that there are two solutions to this dilemma. One is called "relativism." Relativism means believing that not just observation but reality is dependent on theory. To a relativist, the world is different to each person, so that there is no single reality to describe. ["Linguistic relativists" such as Benjamin Lee Whorf (1941) claim that the world is different not for each person but for each language community.] The best that relativist social scientists can do is to try to describe the everyday theories particular people use in particular interactions, making no generalizations (at least no explicit ones) about whether interaction would work the same way in other cases.

The solution Cameron et al. (1992) propose is not relativism but what they call "realism." They acknowledge that *observation* is theory laden (and must accordingly be handled with full awareness that one person's observations may not be the same as another's), but claim that *reality* is not. There are real things happening: people move muscles, utter sounds, and create written records. What people make of a sentence may differ and mishearings are possible, but on some level the experience of two people who hear the same utterance is the same.

Most sociolinguists probably take more or less the same position as Cameron and her colleagues—not positivist but not radically relativist—though not always explicitly, and often without thinking through the implications of their position for their research methods. For example, if observations are believed to be colored by expectations, then it is important to find ways to minimize this as much as possible. One technique might be to get a variety of people to make the observations. Another might be to make the observations a variety of ways. If a researcher's aim is to describe people's sociolinguistic worlds, then it is important to try to get at the theories that color their observations and actions.

There are many ways to collect linguistic data, from observing ongoing interaction or reading written texts to setting up experiments. Wallace Chafe (1994, pp. 17–21) systematizes the possibilities into four categories. Observation, Chafe observes, can be manipulated (the linguist makes something happen) or natural (something happens independent of the linguist), public (based on something the linguist sees) or private (based on what goes on in the linguist's head). Three of the four possible combinations will be discussed in this book. Observation that is natural and private would include the casual introspection involved in reading literature or daydreaming or mentally analyzing one's own thoughts and experiences (see Chapter 6). Natural, public observation would include participant observation and much discourse analysis (see Chapters 7 and 8). Public, manipulated observation includes experimentation and elicitation, both of which are sometimes employed in sociolinguistics, and interviewing, which is common. Private, manipulated observation is involved in syntacticians' making acceptability decisions about sentences or in judgments about constructed examples. Of the four possibilities, this is probably the least common in sociolinguistics, although constructed data (made-up, could-be-real sentences or conversations) are sometimes used.

What Does "Empirical" Mean?

"Empirical" is another word that can be offputting to people who have always liked poems better than petri dishes. But literary study is every bit as empirical as biochemistry: "empirical" simply means "based on observation." The adjective "empirical" should not be

confused with the noun "empiricism," the word for the epistemological theory according to which all knowledge is the result of
observation, a newborn human being a "tabula rasa," or empty slate,
onto which knowledge is written through experience. It is perfectly
possible to be a mentalist, to believe, in other words, that inborn
mental capacities help structure experience and create knowledge,
and still do empirical work. Since sociolinguistics is always based
on observation of one kind or another—it is not a purely introspective discipline like philosophy or mathematics—it is always
empirical, and accordingly the term rarely needs to be used.

What Makes a Good Research Question?

Newcomers to sociolinguistics often find the studies they read fascinating but cannot imagine how they could ever come up with a
research project. They would not know where to start. The starting point for sociolinguistic research (as for research in any area) is
what classical rhetoricians called "invention," the development of
a topic. This section provides some advice about topic development
in sociolinguistics.

Readers of this book who have taught or taken first-year composition already know that a good library research paper is always
based on a clear thesis. Freshman-composition students who say "I'm
going to write my paper about nuclear energy" are told to narrow,
to focus, to develop a point of view. Likewise, effective sociolinguistic research is based on clear research questions. A person who
starts out with the idea of "doing something about language and
gender" or "studying how people talk where I work" will quickly be
overwhelmed by the amount of work that has already been done
and by the variety of things still waiting to be done. In this section
I will illustrate how effective research questions come to be by
describing three projects, two developed by graduate students and
one by a team consisting of two professors and a student. The process
worked somewhat differently in each case.

*Ethnic Identity and Language Use by Women in the Immigrant
Malaysian–Bengali Community* is the title of a Texas A&M Ph.D.
dissertation by Dipika Mukherjee (1995). Mukherjee is an Indian
of Bengali origin who, because of her father's position in the Indian
diplomatic corps, spent parts of her childhood in various foreign

countries. One of these countries was Malaysia. Though Mukherjee and her family were temporary residents of Malaysia, during their 4 years there they were involved with the community of Bengalis who had migrated permanently. Mukherjee made friends with a number of Malaysian–Bengali girls in high school and met her future husband, also a member of the Malaysian–Bengali community. After obtaining her B.A. and M.A. in India, Mukherjee returned to Malaysia, leaving again for her Ph.D. work in the United States.

Partly because she is multilingual, Mukherjee started the Ph.D. program with an interest in bilingualism, and her graduate-school training got her interested in sociolinguistics, in particular, in issues of codeswitching and code-choice. When the time came to select a dissertation topic, she decided that the Malaysian–Bengali community she was already familiar with would be a good site for a study of language and identity. In the first draft of her dissertation proposal, Mukherjee described what she would do this way:

> The purpose of this study is to collect data and analyze language use in a multicultural polyglot community and to test whether the notions about language and society that were developed in more homogeneous societies remain valid here.

This was a promising start, but members of Mukherjee's dissertation committee considered it too broad and unfocused, particularly because Mukherjee would have a limited amount of time in which to "collect data" and "analyze language use." She was asked to pose some more specific questions as well, and she did. The questions were in three sets, two sets about language and identity and one about codeswitching:

1. How do members of this multilingual community use language? Is language used as a device for negotiating identity in the Malaysian–Bengali community in Malaysia?
2. How important is group identity among the members in this community? How does linguistic variability correlate with integration into this group, and in the larger Malaysian context? Does this network work as a norm-enforcement mechanism? Does peer pressure affect language choice more than the family in this community? Is ethnic identity separate from language identity for the members of this immigrant community?

3. Is codeswitching valued in this society or discouraged? Who codeswitches more, women or men, the young or the old? Do women codeswitch more using Bengali as the matrix language? Do men use more English in their speech?

Thinking of all the questions she might like to answer was a fruitful step for Mukherjee. It allowed her and her committee members to suggest ways the questions could be combined and to clarify various possibilities for research subjects and particular topics. In the process it became obvious that many of the questions overlapped, and that it might make sense to focus on the group that would be most likely to need ways of expressing complex multiethnic identities. Mukherjee was interested in code-choice as it related to ethnic identity. The language that was most likely to be used to express Malaysian–Bengalis' ethnic identity was Bengali, although it would also be important to examine uses of English, Malaysian, and the languages in which they communicated with household servants. The people Mukherjee knew best in the community and had easiest access to were women—her friends, their mothers and grandmothers, and their younger relatives—and women seemed to be in charge of the community's ethnic heritage in a way men were not.

The final draft of Mukherjee's proposal posed her research question this way:

> How do different women in this multilingual Malaysian–Bengali immigrant community use the Bengali language to negotiate identity?

Together with this question was a description of what Mukherjee would do during her year of fieldwork:

> I will focus on the language choice of twelve women in the immigrant Malaysian–Bengali community in Malaysia. . . . I will focus on the functional, rather than the structural, aspect of codeswitching and code-choice. This study will largely be an ethnography of communication and combine additional methodological approaches including case-studies, discourse and narrative analysis, and interviews. . . . A questionnaire/interview, two hours of speech recording of each informant at family dinners, and participant observation will constitute the data. The focus

of the analysis will be to explore audience, setting and topic effect on the negotiation of identity through code-choice.

This research plan was useful to Mukherjee in several ways. For one thing, it helped her stay focused on collecting the data she needed to suggest an answer to her research question, a task that was not easy, since during her fieldwork year she was also teaching full time and raising two young children. The complexity of her research site also made it important to have a clear question in mind and a clear plan for approaching it. There were hundreds of things about the Malaysian–Bengali community that would have been worth studying and many temptations to change topics or get sidetracked. Furthermore, Mukherjee's previous work as a journalist had accustomed her to short projects with strict time limits, and large projects such as this could be overwhelming and could induce panic. So being able to refer to her research question helped her stay calmer and more organized.

Heidi Ehernberger Hamilton took a different approach to developing a research focus, doing so as she analyzed her data rather than before collecting it. Her study, published in 1994 as *Conversations With an Alzheimer's Patient,* also began as a dissertation. Early in her graduate career, Hamilton's Georgetown University professors began to encourage her to think about real-world applications for the ideas about sociolinguistics she was exploring in classes, and she turned, naturally, to a situation in which she was already involved, her work in the nursing home in which she was a volunteer. The first term project she did involved tracking the speech acts in which patients and staff engaged on their way to and from exercise classes, showing that it was useful to get people out of their rooms, because this got them to interact with others. Eventually, the institution's volunteer coordinator matched Hamilton with an elderly woman with Alzheimer's disease whom she called Elsie. By this point Hamilton was interested more specifically in the dementia associated with Alzheimer's and how it affected language skills.

Although Elsie was physically coordinated and did not look unusual, non-Alzheimer's residents of the nursing home found her frightening because she talked in an unusual way. Hamilton was interested in exploring what was unusual about Elsie's talk, and, noticing that Elsie's linguistic and communicative abilities were changing over time, Hamilton wanted to track the changes, too.

These interests were reflected in Hamilton's dissertation proposal, in which she explored the meager research literature on naturalistic studies of Alzheimer's disease, realizing that sociolinguists had written very little on the topic. Hamilton's professors encouraged her not to decide in advance what she would look for in her data, stressing the possibility that having preset analytical categories might cause her to miss other important and interesting facets of the conversations she had taped with Elsie. So Hamilton's proposal suggested that the problems she would be studying seemed to have to do with a lack of coherence in the conversations and that there were some pragmatic problems involving things such as making appropriate responses to questions, but her plan was to let her study be "data-driven," "allowing the conversational data themselves to lead [her] to [her] frameworks and working hypotheses" (Hamilton, 1994, p. 29).

As she began to read through her transcripts, Hamilton noted anything that seemed unusual about the conversations in the margins. She knew her data were rich, but not yet exactly why. Eventually, though, her marginal notations began to group together into categories to which Hamilton could give names. Some of the odd features of the conversations seemed to have to do with relatively nonautomatic aspects of talk (more formulaic, often-performed procedures were easier than creative ones) and other features could be attributed to problems involving taking the other speaker's perspective. The names Hamilton had available for her categories, and the explanatory frameworks associated with these names, came from things she had read in classes and on her own and learned at conferences. Someone with different training might have come up with different, perhaps just as useful ways of talking about what was going wrong in the conversations. Hamilton eventually decided that in order to track changes in the conversations over time it would be useful to focus on how she and Elsie responded to each other's questions. Responses could be counted; the sorts of troubles in which she was interested could be seen in them; responses collected in controlled interview settings had been studied by other researchers, so her results could be compared with theirs.

The third project whose development we will explore was more limited in scope than the two dissertation projects. It resulted in a journal article, "Gender, Politeness, and Discourse Management in Same-Sex and Cross-Sex Opinion-Poll Interviews" by Kathleen Ferrara, Judith Mattson Bean, and me (Johnstone et al., 1992). It was a new project for all of us (two professors and a graduate student). Although we were all interested in language and gender, none of us had worked with these data before and none of us was a specialist in the area. Ferrara and I wanted to do a joint project, and there was money available to hire Bean to work with us.

The data, tapes of telephone public-opinion survey interviews, had been collected by a colleague of ours for another purpose. At his suggestion, we had listened to some of the tapes to see how they might be useful in our work on narratives and conversations, and we and others (including some students doing class projects) had transcribed some of them. When we started thinking about the interviews, we had no particular research question in mind, although we realized that these highly constrained, partly scripted conversations were potentially of great interest. They were verbal interactions that were as controlled as could be but still completely natural, not set up for our research purposes. Each set of interlocutors— interviewer and respondent—had the same anonymous relationship with one another, and they talked about the same things, in almost the same order, for the same reasons.

One of the things that struck us on first listening to the tapes was how varied they turned out to be. Some were 20 minutes long and consisted mainly of the interviewer's asking questions almost exactly as they appeared on the script and the interviewee's answering them exactly the way she was supposed to, with choices the interviewer gave her or in short phrases. Others were more than 45 minutes long and included flirtation, laughter, jokes, objections to the job, apologies, long explanations of why respondents were answering as they were, and other departures from the task at hand. Most were somewhere in between. The questions we asked at that early stage were very general: "Why aren't these interviews more similar?" and "Why don't the speakers stick to the job?"

Neither of these would have made a good research topic, since they neither define their terms clearly (what constitutes "similar" or "sticking to the job," for example?) nor suggest how the questions might be answered. (Would the answer to "Why don't the speakers stick to the job" come from interviews with the speakers, from an analysis of what they were doing instead of sticking to the job, or from a comparison of their behavior in this speech event with their behavior in another?) Two of the first tapes we heard were one of the shortest and most businesslike and one of the longest and most verbose. The interviewers in both cases were women; the respondent in the first was a woman and the respondent in the second was a man. The woman behaved like many women the three of us knew and the man like many men we knew. This almost inevitably made us wonder whether gender had something to do with the heterogeneity of the interviews.

As Ferrara and I thought more about the interviews and listened to the ones that had been transcribed, we noticed several relevant things. Almost all the interviewers were women (of the 24 who had administered that run of the survey, 22 were female), so we decided we would need to concentrate on this large subset of the interviews. It turned out to be the case that the interviews with female respondents were indeed more likely to be brief and stay on task, though there were deviations from the scripted job in every interview. Interviewers talking to men seemed often to turn the task into a game in some way, by adopting a sort of game-show hostess delivery, for example, whereas in the interviews with women the respondents often talked about the task as if it were a test. Male respondents often seemed to be trying to find clever ways to deviate from the interview job, which interviewers would acknowledge by laughing. At that point we asked ourselves a more specific question: "What is the relationship between gender-marked kinds of talk in the interviews and the sex of the respondents?" For a conference paper, we proposed an answer to this question by looking for examples of what O'Barr and Atkins (1980) called "powerless talk"—features that they found characterized the speech of the people in an interaction with less power over conversational topics and turntaking, such as defendants in a courtroom. We looked at 44 interviews, half with women and half with men. We found that there was more powerless talk by interviewers when respondents were men, and we speculated that this might be a way interviewers manipulated relative power and status in the interview in order to get respondents to complete the task without feeling imposed on.

Having started to think about the interviews in terms of politeness (how to keep people from feeling imposed on), we decided to explore a more systematic way of comparing interviews with men with interviews with women. We asked, "Do interviewers' expressions of politeness differ depending on whether they are talking to women or to men?" and "If so, how and why?" Using a well-known list of "politeness strategies" (Brown and Levinson, 1987), Bean set out to identify which ones interviewers used in which interviews. She soon noticed, though, that politeness was not the only reason interviewers departed from their scripts. Many departures had instead to do with what we called "discourse management," the job of keeping the interview on track (making sure respondents understood the questions, telling them the correct formats for answering, getting back on task after interruptions, and so on). We added discourse management to our research question: "Do interviewers' expressions of politeness and discourse management differ depending on whether they are talking to women or to men?" and "If so, how and why?"

As they appeared in the paper we wrote about the study, our research questions were these (Johnstone et al., 1992, p. 150):

1) Do the female interviewers use different politeness strategies with the male respondents than with the female respondents? 2) Do the female interviewers use different discourse management techniques with the female respondents than with the male respondents? 3) If there are differences, what appears to account for them?

If these questions are compared to our original formulation—"Why aren't these interviews more similar?" and "Why don't the speakers stick to the job?"—their advantages are clear. For questions 1 and 2, we had specified exactly what we meant by "the interviews," "politeness strategies," and "discourse management techniques" (and "male" and "female" were also unambiguous in this context), so it was clear precisely what would constitute an answer to each question. The answer to question 3 would be more speculative, as we indicated by using "appears." Although this set of questions would probably be too specific for a dissertation, it was the right size for a paper in which we claimed only to have found an interesting way to shed some light on one aspect of language and gender. (We eventually did several other studies of the interview data, approaching our initial curiosity about their heterogeneity in other ways.)

What generalizations can we make about effective research questions on the basis of these three examples? For one thing, a well-focused research topic can generally be phrased as a question or a series of closely related questions, as it was in the Malaysian–

Bengali study and the survey interview study. It is sometimes helpful, in fact, in the process of finding a topic, to formulate your idea as
a question. A workable question is one the researcher knows how to
go about answering; it is wise to think about exactly what procedures
you have in mind when you use terms such as "look at" or "examine"
or "describe" and to make sure you can define all the words in your
question in such a way as to be able to "know one if you saw it."

Research questions are not always formulated in advance of data
collection, as the Alzheimer's and public-opinion survey examples
show. There is nothing wrong with using data that were not collected with a specific question in mind, as long as there is something interesting, significant, and timely that the data can help
reveal. Given plenty of time and, for students, help from teachers,
letting data "speak for itself" may eventually result in a richer set
of questions and answers than a more controlled, preplanned design.
The researcher's focus can narrow gradually, in the process of thinking about, listening to, or reading the data or talking to potential
research subjects.

The two dissertation studies emphasize the importance of working with something that is familiar. Mukherjee was wise to choose
to do her work in a community in which she partly grew up, as was
Hamilton in working with a woman and in a setting she had known
for several years. But the study by Johnstone et al. shows that it is
possible to work with unfamiliar material, as long as what is potentially important about it can be seen. We learned about survey interviewing as we went along. In every case, work should involve material that is easily available. Sociolinguists are lucky in that we rarely
have to look too hard for something interesting to study.

Our three examples illustrate another aspect of topic development: it is wise to choose ways of working that are enjoyable and
at which you are good. Different researchers have different strengths.
For example, Mukherjee's choice of a mainly ethnographic approach
suited her in that she enjoyed talking to people and was unselfconscious about asking them questions. Hamilton liked older people and was good at drawing people like Elsie out, so she could collect useful data from someone who did not talk much. Bean enjoyed
detailed analysis but preferred to be told exactly how to do it, so
our eventual selection of an approach that involved lists of coding
choices (politeness and discourse-management strategies) and an
easy way of identifying parts of the interviews that needed to be

---

Box 3.1   What Makes a Workable Research Topic?

Your project may not meet all these criteria, but unless most are met you may have trouble.

- A well-focused idea can be phrased as a question or a set of closely related questions. (Your questions may become narrower in the course of your research, but you must have clear questions with which to start.)
- You know how you will go about answering the questions, that is, what your research methodology or methodologies will be.
- You can describe why the questions are important in a wider context: why answering them will have practical value in the profession and/or the world at large.
- You (or the leader of your research team) are familiar with the research site.
- You have access to the research site.
- You have the time it will realistically take to carry out the research, analyze the results, and write your report. It can be useful to make a timeline for yourself.
- The project requires ways of collecting and analyzing data with which you are comfortable and at which you are competent.

---

labeled was a good one. Some people find it easy to approach strangers and ask to tape-record them, whereas others would find this very difficult; some people are better at noticing small details and others better at noticing big trends. Develop a research question that is not only answerable but that *you* could answer.

What Is "Qualitative" Research?

In the survey-interview study described in the previous section, we asked questions whose answers would include numbers. After coding

each departure from the interview script with the name of a politeness or discourse-management strategy, we counted how many there
were of each in each interview. Then we averaged the figures for each
strategy across interviews with female respondents and across interviews with male respondents. We compared these figures, using a statistical test to see if the differences were significant (that is, highly
unlikely to have been the result if the strategy categories had been
assigned randomly). This gave us answers to our first two questions.

    This use of numbers means that the interview study is at least
partly quantitative. The Malaysian–Bengali study was qualitative
rather than quantitative. Mukherjee's questions were about *how* and
why Bengali and other languages were used, not about *how often*
Bengali was used in her data or *how much* of it was used. To answer
these questions, she found instances of the use of Bengali, Malaysian
English, and so on, and, using insights she had gained from talking
with her research subjects, proposed reasons for the uses of each language. For instance, she observed that among the youngest women
she studied, "knowledge of Bengali is flaunted and a lack of knowledge derided in a bantering way," while the unmarked language
choice for these women is Malaysian English. She supported this
claim with an example that illustrates both the use of Bengali, transcribed in italics and glossed, and the use of Malaysian English features, in boldface (Mukherjee, 1995, p. 170):

TANU: It's [the food] good isn't it?

LATA: *Ki shundo.* [mispronounced]
        (*How beautiful.*)

TANU: Not *shundor, ki shundor* means beautiful.

LATA: Okay, or *ki bhalo.* [laughter all around]
        (*Okay or how good.*)
        "Heh-heh." [mimicking others' laughter] **Act natural lah
        you idiot.**

TANU: [laughs] **Acting-lah idiot you.**

    The answers to the questions Hamilton asked in the Alzheimer's
study were arrived at sometimes with qualitative analyses and sometimes via quantification. Hamilton counted, for example, how many
of her responses to questions and how many of Elsie's were appropriate in the context, and made these figures into percentages for

each time they met. (Hamilton was careful to "operationalize" the term *appropriate*, describing the criteria by which appropriate responses would be distinguished from inappropriate ones.) During their March 1984 meeting, for example, Hamilton's responses were appropriate 74% of the time whereas Elsie's were appropriate 39% of the time (Hamilton, 1994, pp. 115, 131). To show that Elsie was able to use linguistic attention-getters even when her disease was fairly advanced, Hamilton used an example (p. 62):

> ELSIE: They have they're have to get to get together, honey dear. And they have to get. *Listen, dear honey.*
> HEIDI: Yes, what?

Hamilton's use of both kinds of questions—about how much and how often and about how and why—illustrates that sociolinguistic research projects are neither exclusively quantitative nor exclusively qualitative. They are most often both.

Equally important, sociolinguistic work is always "interpretive," whether the interpretation involves numbers or results of some other kind. To interpret something—an event, a verbal pattern, a set of numbers—is to decide what it means. Uninterpreted data are "raw" data; they do not confirm or disconfirm any hypothesis. Only with interpretation does an analysis have a point. Thus it is always necessary to interpret the data and the results of the analysis, whatever approach is taken. The contrast between sociolinguistics that is relatively quantitative (such as the work reported in the journal *Language Variation and Change*) and sociolinguistics that is relatively qualitative (such as much of the work in *Language in Society*) lies in whether research questions are answered via relatively mechanical procedures (counting, calculating averages, performing statistical tests to see which factors vary systematically together or how likely results are to be random) or relatively nonmechanical ones (asking people about things, watching, listening). But deciding what to count in what category always involves interpretation. This was true of the survey-interview study, for example, in which each departure from the script had to be identified as an instance of one or another politeness or discourse-management strategy. Conversely, deciding when enough has been seen or heard to come to a conclusion always involves counting, explicitly or not. If she had observed young women showing off their Bengali only once, Mukherjee could have not made the claim she did.

Summary

Research involves systematic attempts to find out the answers to questions. Sociolinguistic work usually combines literature searches (through which we find out what others have discovered about the topic) with data collection involving systematic observations of one kind or another. Observations are not always (and may never be) completely trustworthy, so we need ways of ensuring that we are doing all we can to observe from different perspectives and in different ways. A manageable research project must be based on clear, well-designed research questions, and much of this chapter has consisted of a set of examples of how research topics can be developed. The analysis phase of sociolinguistic research is often quantitative as well as qualitative. This means that analyzing sociolinguistic data often involves some counting, explicit or implicit, in order to answer questions about how often things happen, in addition to the descriptions that help answer qualitative questions about how and why things happen.

Discussion Questions

1. Imagine that you had each of the following sets of data. Develop one or more sociolinguistic research questions you could ask about each, and decide how you could go about answering the questions.
   a. Tapes of interactions between customers and salespeople in franchise mall stores (earring booths, 1-hour photo places, etc.).
   b. The diary of a seventeenth-century English religious reformer describing her travels and travails.
   c. Transcripts (made by people whose spelling was often phonetic) of interviews with Civil War veterans from Tennessee.

    d. Videotapes of graduate students and faculty members teaching sections of freshman composition or introductory linguistics.

2. One question that was not asked in this chapter is "What is science?" What do you suppose the reason for this omission was?

    a. Sociolinguistics is not science.

    b. Sociolinguistics is obviously science.

    c. It doesn't matter whether sociolinguistics is science.

Argue for your choice.

Suggestions for Further Reading

A useful source of ideas about invention—systematically analyzing a topic and formulating research questions—is Young et al. (1970).

◆ 4 ◆

Some Legal and Ethical Issues

People who write and publish novels or poems expect their work to be analyzed and critiqued. Novels and poems are performances, and performed speech, as Bauman (1977), Pratt (1977), and others have argued, is precisely speech that is open to analysis and evaluation, speech whose form, as well as its content, is supposed to matter. But speakers and writers who are *not* consciously performing have not made the same implicit contract with people who hear or read their words. Most of the time people who speak or write are not agreeing to have their words criticized or analyzed, or indeed even remembered.

Much sociolinguistic research (unlike, say, literary criticism) uses relatively nonperformed discourse as data. (We sometimes refer to this as "everyday" or "vernacular" language.) Sociolinguists are thus in danger of breaching a basic unspoken agreement when they record and analyze talk that is not usually understood as being available for critique. This chapter is about some of the issues that arise as a result of the unusual relationship between linguists and the people they study, as well as some related issues involving who does the work, who pays for it, and the purpose for which it is used. We begin by thinking about the relationship between researchers and "researched." Is it ever right to record people without their knowledge? What is "informed consent"? When is anonymity crucial? How should the people we study be involved in our work? We then consider the relationship between researchers and the other sorts of resources they sometimes need: money and assistants. In what ways can and in what ways should funding sources affect research designs?

How should research assistants be selected and how should they be treated? Finally, we discuss some ethical issues involving research results, thinking about the agendas, overt and covert, that structure sociolinguists' work.

Researchers and Researched

Much of the casual noticing that gives rise to research topics is based on surreptitious observation: the people being observed are not aware of the observation. As we listen to people talking or read people's writing or watch them sign, in the normal course of daily events, sociolinguists sometimes notice not just what others are saying but how they are saying it. Our training encourages us to take perspectives others may not take: we notice things such as nonreciprocal uses of terms of address, gendered predilections for conversational behavior, and syntactic parallelism. We may only wish that, like Henry Higgins in Shaw's *Pygmalion*, we could identify a person's place of origin after overhearing a sentence or two, but we can sometimes create a conversational stir by voicing a metalinguistic observation of some other kind: "Do you know what you just said?"

Sociolinguistic party tricks like this catch people off guard. People who find out that they have been surreptitiously studied in this casual way often find it amusing, but they are also often made uneasy, even if the observation was just for fun and even if the observer was a friend. This unease is at the root of legal and ethical issues involving surreptitious recording and informed consent.

Although surreptitious *observation*, at least in public, is not controversial—people are always watching and overhearing one another, and it can be argued that people expect to be watched and overheard in public settings—surreptitious *recording* of talk or writing that is not explicitly public has been the subject of debate. In the United States as elsewhere, there are statues and case-law precedents that bear on the legality of "bugging" other people's conversations and of using conversations bugged by other people as data. As Labov (1972a) and others have pointed out, people sometimes talk differently if they know their talk is being recorded. Sociolinguists who want to study people's most unselfconscious, "vernacular" speech have to find ways to simulate, on tape, a situation in which the observer and the tape recorder are not there. Recording people without their knowledge is tempting under these circumstances, and in some places and with some restrictions it may not be illegal. (Where surreptitious recording is legal, it is usually restricted to situations in which one party to the recorded conversation knows about the recording.) Many of the specific statutes regarding surreptitious recording are untested in court, and, in any case, the law changes quickly.

Although it may be tempting to study people who do not know that they are being studied, surreptitious recording raises ethical as well as legal questions. It is deceptive, for one thing. There are research techniques in sociolinguistics in which deception of a certain kind is crucial: one example is the matched-guise technique, which, in its classic form, uses the voice of one person speaking in two different languages or varieties, played to research subjects who are led to believe they are listening to two different people. But although even this sort of deceptiveness could be called into question, it seems considerably more benign than the deceptiveness involved in surreptitious recording. This has to do in part with the fact that surreptitious recording risks violating people's privacy, if they are saying things they did not mean others to hear. In any case, many sociolinguists would prefer not to objectify people by studying them as if they were atoms or ants. Precisely because humans can talk and reflect, it may be not only fair but advantageous to involve research subjects in research, in one way or another.

Box 4.1   Surreptitious Recording?

If you are thinking of recording people surreptitiously, make sure that what you do to obtain the recordings would be likely to be considered legal in a court of law. Sources that were up to date when they were published are Murray and Murray (1992, 1996), and, on the use of data surreptitiously collected by others, Shuy (1986). Unless there are very compelling reasons for it, surreptitious recording is not a good idea. In many situations, it is illegal.

One way in which research subjects are often required to be involved in research projects is via "informed consent" procedures. Most universities require grant applicants and thesis or dissertation writers to specify procedures by which they will inform human research subjects of what a study is about and how it will be conducted and to obtain their consent, represented by their signatures. Dissertation and thesis research that does not meet institutional human-subjects requirements may be rejected. This can apply even to research papers for courses. Human-subjects reviews are particularly rigorous for research in which people may be exposed to risk. Since the sorts of things sociolinguists do—tape-recording people's talk in relatively naturalistic situations, having them complete attitude questionnaires, and asking them to tell stories or describe their neighborhoods—are usually not seen as involving physical, mental, or legal risk to subjects, sociolinguists are not always required by their institutions to follow formal informed consent procedures, and they do not always do so on their own if they are not required to. Often it seems easier, and less likely to make people awkwardly self-conscious, simply to ask if it is okay to record, without going into detail and without getting each individual's permission individually, or even to record first and ask later.

In some cases this procedure, informal consent rather than truly informed consent, may be adequate. But it has some potential drawbacks. Getting a group's permission, rather than each individual's, may mask the fact that some people in the group are not as comfortable with the situation as others but are reluctant to cause a stir or risk peer disapproval by saying so. People's reactions to tape recorders and video cameras vary widely, so it is hard to generalize, but people do sometimes forget that they are being recorded and so should sometimes be asked for consent again after the recording is over. Informal ways of eliciting consent may also cause problems later, if the researcher decides to continue with the project after the initial study is over and then needs informed consent from people who are no longer available. And, unpleasant though it may be, sociolinguists need to think about legal liability. A person whose consent was not individually sought and to whom the research project was not carefully explained could make a stronger case in court for personal injury as a result of the research than could someone who was really informed. Larmouth (1992) provides a more detailed discussion of consent procedures as they apply to linguistic research, and is worth reading for anyone with doubts about how to proceed.

Informed consent involves several things. In the words of one good overview (Lindlof, 1995):

> Anyone who participates in study should (a) do so voluntarily, (b) be able to understand what the study demands of him or her, (c) be able to understand participation's risks and benefits, and (d) have the legal capacity to give consent. . . . Even if they consent, they can leave the study at any time without negative consequences. (p. 99)

Lindlof's sample consent form (pp. 100–101) describes the purpose of the research, its duration and procedures, risks and discomforts and benefits for potential subjects, compensation (if subjects are not to be paid, this is made clear too), and procedures for ensuring confidentiality.

The issue of confidentiality can be problematic for sociolinguists, since we often audiotape or videotape people, which makes their identities potentially recoverable even if they are given pseudonyms. But unless there is a clear understanding to the contrary between you and your subjects, or unless you are studying public figures or truly public speech—speech that is broadcast or printed, meant to be evaluated and meant to be attributed to its author—you need to make your research subjects anonymous or pseudonymous. Even though a research presentation at a colloquium or conference may be more lively and better illustrated with a bit of tape, if there is a chance of people's recognizing voices or faces it may be better not to play it, and it is always wise not only to change names on transcripts but to erase or record over them on the tapes and to edit published transcripts and change descriptions of research situations enough so that the identity of participants could not be determined.

The specific wording of an informed consent document, as well as the level of detail that is appropriate, depends on the nature of the research project. A fairly simple format is the one Judith Mattson Bean and I used in our case-study research about women from Texas. (For a slightly adapted version, see Sample 4.1.)

Sample 4.1   Certification of Informed Consent

Professors Barbara Johnstone and Judith Mattson Bean are carrying out a study of Texas women's speech. As part of the study, they will audiotape interviews with nine women, of whom I will be one. Drs. Johnstone and Bean have discussed the project with me. The project will result in publications in academic journals and, it is hoped, eventually in a book in which my speech may be quoted, described, and analyzed. If I have provided other materials relating to myself, my work, or my speech, or if other materials are publicly available, these materials may also be quoted, described, and analyzed. The intent of the study is to describe Texas women's speech, not to evaluate it.

By signing this form, I certify that Drs. Johnstone and Bean's research project has been satisfactorily explained to me and that I consent to participate in it in the ways described above.

Name: _____

Signature: _____

Date: _____

We were explicitly interested in studying public discourse by public figures; some of them were so well known that their identities would be impossible to disguise, and some others saw the publicity we might generate as a benefit to them. As a result, we did not promise them anonymity, although we have, in fact, used pseudonyms in our publications where it was possible and when we thought the participants preferred it. On the form, we reminded the participants of what we were doing and how they would be involved (we had discussed the project with each woman previously, in arranging to meet with her), and we set out, in general terms, what we would be doing with the data we collected and why. Then we asked each to sign her name to the consent statement, certifying that the project had been explained to her satisfaction. In addition to this, we began each interview—with the tape recorder running—by explaining our project again and asking the interviewee whether she had questions about it.

A considerably more detailed format is the one Mary Bucholtz (1997) used in her dissertation study of high-school students. Partly because she was working with young people, a considerably more vulnerable, powerless population than the women Bean and I studied, and asking them about more intimate things than we asked our participants about, Bucholtz's document is more explicit about the nature of the conversations she planned to have with the young people, about her procedures for recording and for preserving anonymity, and about the uses to which her data might be put. (See Sample 4.2.)

Sample 4.2   Certification of Informed Consent

My name is Mary Bucholtz. I am a graduate student at the University of California at Berkeley. I would like you to take part in my research on the language of friendship among teenagers and young adults. I want to find out how people talk about friendship, and how they talk to their friends.

If you and your parent(s) or guardian(s) agree that you may participate in the research, I will meet you at [your high school] during your lunch hour or at another time and place that we agree on. There I will talk to you for about thirty minutes about your friendships at your school and what you think about friendship generally. I will record our interview on a tape-recorder and I may ask you to wear a small clip-on microphone during the recording.

After our interview, I may want to talk to you in more detail, with some of your friends. I will ask all of you about what you like to do together, what you like about each other, and how you became friends. I may also ask to meet with you and your friends outside of school to get an idea of how you talk to each other when you are relaxing together. I may ask to tape-record some of these conversations; if I do, I may again ask you to wear a clip-on microphone.

During the interview(s), I may ask you who you like and dis-like, and who you think others like and dislike. I may also find out other private things about your life if I later meet with you and your friends. You may not want others to find out these things, so I will protect your privacy in every way I can:

- I will not let other people listen to the tapes or read tran-scripts or notes based on our conversation(s) unless you give your permission for them to do so. I will keep the tapes and writings locked up in a safe place in my home, where only I can get to them. I will not tell your friends, teachers, or family members what you say during our conversation(s).

- In writing and talking about my study, I will never use your name or any other names that could give away your iden-tity. You will choose a name that I will use to refer to you. I will also use invented names for other people in your life so that no one can use that information to figure out who you are. Papers with your real name on them—this form and a note to myself reminding me what your invented name is—will be locked up in my home, separately from each other and from the tape-recordings and transcripts. In addition, the note reminding me what your invented name is will have only your first name on it.

- If at any point in the study you want me to erase from the tape anything you've said, you have the right to tell me to do this, and I will erase it in your presence.

After this research is completed, I may save the tape and notes for use in future research. However, I will protect your privacy in the future in the same way that I will protect it during the study.

Your participation in this research is voluntary. You are free to refuse to take part and you may refuse to answer any questions or may stop taking part at any time. Whether or not you partic-ipate will have no effect on your standing at your school.

If you have any questions about the research, you may call me, Mary Bucholtz, at [phone number]. If you and your parent(s) or guardian(s) agree that you may take part in this research, please return a signed copy of this form to me when we meet or send it to [address]. You should keep one copy of this form for your records.

Your signature on each part of the consent form indicates that you give permission for each part of the study. If you are under age 18, one of your parents or guardians must sign each part of the form as well. You may choose to sign only some parts of the form and not others.

1. I agree to take part in this research.

Student signature _____   Date _____
Parent/Guardian signature _____   Date _____

2. I give permission for the tape-recordings to be transcribed. I understand that the transcript will not include any names or details that will give away my identity.

Student signature _____   Date _____
Parent/Guardian signature _____   Date _____

3. I give permission for the transcripts to be used for teaching purposes and for presentation of the research at conferences.

Student signature _____   Date _____
Parent/Guardian signature _____   Date _____

4. I give permission for parts of the tape-recordings to be used for teaching purposes and for presentation of the research at conferences.

Student signature _____   Date _____
Parent/Guardian signature _____   Date _____

Bucholtz's elaboration of the potential risks to the teenagers' privacy makes her consent form look more imposing than ours, but it did not in fact put very many teenagers or their parents or guardians off: most people who were asked were willing to participate fully. Bucholtz told potential participants what they would be talking about, but left the sociolinguistic purpose of her research unspoken, so as to avoid linguistic self-consciousness. Because we were interested, among other things, in how Texans talk about Texas linguistic resources, we did tell our research participants that we would be studying their speech, but not that we would be making systematic efforts to elicit a variety of speech styles during the interview.

If you use published material, you will probably need to get the permission of the copyright holder. You do not generally need permission to *study* published documents, but you often do need permission to *quote* more than a few words of them in reporting about your study. It is worth looking into this early, since it can be annoying to find, when you come to write about your project, that you are not allowed to quote from your data. The law in this area is evolving, too, and you should find out what the current interpretation is.

How explicit does the information we give informed subjects have to be? Researchers are not normally expected to tell their subjects what they are doing at the level of detail required, for example, in a dissertation proposal or a grant application. Not only might this be very difficult, requiring more background lecturing about linguistics than people want to hear, but it might also influence what is found, as subjects try to do what they think is expected (or try *not* to do what they think is expected). Practically speaking, informing subjects means telling them what you are doing in general terms ("describing Texas women's speech," for example) and also what you are not doing, namely evaluating them or their speech. What a researcher says specifically depends a great deal on the researcher's particular project, as we have seen.

The same applies to "debriefing": telling research participants, after the study is over, what its results were. The idea of taking research results back to the research site has a long history in fields such as anthropology, and it is in principle a good idea. Knowing that the people you are studying are going to find out what you have said about them helps keep you scrupulous and sensitive to local understandings of the world, and people may be more likely to trust future researchers if they know that previous ones have kept them informed about their findings. In practice, debriefing may not always be possible, sometimes for practical reasons and sometimes because research participants are not particularly interested.

Informed consent is an ethical as well as a legal requirement: the need to think about our research from the perspective of the people we study does not end once they have explicitly agreed to participate. The extent to which we involve the people we study in our work, at all stages, has to do with how we conceive of our relationship to them. The discussion so far in this chapter has presupposed a fairly traditional view of the relationship between researcher and researched, a view that Cameron et al. (1992) call the "ethical" view. In this paradigm, researchers think carefully about how their research may affect the research subjects (such as by exposing them to risk) and about how to proceed (for example, about how much deception is acceptable, if any) and how to compensate subjects for their participation. But subjects do not affect the researcher's agenda in any basic way: the researcher poses the questions and uses subjects as tools in testing answers. Research is *on* the researched. Most published research in sociolinguistics is of this sort.

In an alternative view, which Cameron et al. call "advocacy," research is not only *on* but also *for* subjects. This way of conceiving of the relationship between researcher and researched sees the researcher as indebted to the people he or she studies and thus required to make research findings available to them for their own use. The example Cameron et al. give of research in this paradigm is William Labov's well-known article on "Objectivity and Commitment in Linguistic Science" (1982). In this paper Labov described the use of his and others' research about what was then called Black English Vernacular in an important lawsuit involving educational discrimination. The advocacy paradigm shares with the ethical paradigm the view that the sociolinguist is the expert and the research subjects the tools, but it differs from the ethical paradigm in encouraging the researcher to use results for the subjects' benefit.

A third way of imagining the relationship between researcher and subjects involves "empowerment." In this view, according to Cameron et al., researchers are obligated not just to defend the people they study, but to involve them. Research in this paradigm is *on, for,* and *with* the researched. This view is based on three assumptions, which Cameron et al. state this way:

a) Persons are not objects and should not be treated as objects.
b) Subjects have their own agendas and research should try to address them.
c) If knowledge is worth having, it is worth sharing. (pp. 23–24)

As ethnographers have long observed, people's own understandings of what they are doing constitute part of reality, and although Cameron et al. stop short of suggesting that researchers should accordingly simply let subjects speak for themselves, they make it clear that research subjects have a role to play in explaining what they do and in posing the questions that research about them should try to answer. Sociolinguists tend to assume that because people are not good at reporting the details of their pronunciation, they will also be poor reporters of their linguistic behavior on other levels. This is sometimes true, and certainly people's reports and explanations of their behavior, linguistic and otherwise, can be heavily colored by folk theories about what people ought to do. In some situations, though, people are remarkably self-aware about language; they know what they are doing.

Practically speaking, what are the implications of taking the empowerment view? Dialectologists have always included research subjects in data *collection,* asking them what "people say around here," for example. More explicit attempts to involve subjects in data collection include, for example, that of Shirley Brice Heath (1983, pp. 263–342), whose "teachers as learners" and school-aged "learners as ethnographers" studied the communities of which they were part. The ways participation benefitted Heath's research subjects were obvious in their teaching and in their school success. More recent "action research" in schools and prisons embeds data collection in educational or therapeutic activities and makes all participants data collectors. For example, in O'Connor's (1995) work on personal narratives by men in a maximum-security prison, some of the data were generated during a classroom activity in which they planned for a drama workshop, and other stories were elicited in the explicit attempt by O'Connor to encourage the men to think about themselves as agents of their actions.

One technique that involves research subjects in *interpreting* the data is "playback" (Schultz and Erikson, 1982; Tannen, 1984, pp. 37–38) or "feedback" (Rampton, 1992): having subjects or people like them (or both) listen to tapes of themselves or look at the results of linguistic tasks they did and comment on what was happening or why. This necessarily involves making sure that research subjects understand the questions you are asking, so it means that consent is as informed as it can be. It has the advantage of showing the researcher how subjects and people like them feel about the issues being addressed in the research, and the feedback process can provide additional information for analysis.

How playback or feedback procedures benefit research subjects depends on who they are and what the project is; in most cases it can at least help people see themselves in a new and perhaps useful way and give them a way of talking about their sociolinguistic behavior. Sometimes, of course, the people you are studying simply are not interested in your findings and have no use for them (Harvey, 1992, gives an example). Sometimes, too, they may want to use your results for different purposes than you would expect or choose. (An example of my own involved a woman who publicly announced the fact that she and someone much more famous than she had both been part of a study of mine, as a way of advertising herself.) Empowering research subjects implies disempowering the researcher, at least potentially; some sociolinguists welcome this, though, and all should think about the possibility of involving the people being studied.

Researchers and Resources

Sociolinguistic researchers often need assistance, and this, along with other things about fieldwork, costs money. These facts raise some potential problems. It has become almost traditional in large sociolinguistic projects for graduate students to provide most of the research assistance, sometimes helping design the project but more often following procedures set by the principal investigators, who are also their faculty mentors; student fieldworkers then get to use the data they and others have collected as the basis for theses and dissertations. Arranging things this way gives students a leg up in the academic job market, since by the time they graduate they will probably have been co-presenter of parts of the larger project and co-author of reports about it. Student fieldworkers see firsthand how projects are designed and methodologies worked out, and, because the students' own research reports in the form of their M.A. or Ph.D. work represent part of the results of their mentors' projects, mentors are motivated to be insistent that this work is rigorous and well grounded.

When this way of working is congenial to principal investigator and student fieldworker alike, it benefits both. But there are risks involved. The advantages of being part of someone else's project have to be weighed against the advantages of trying to answer the questions that got you into sociolinguistics in the first place, which may not be exactly the questions your professors are asking. The practical advantage of working on a more or less set topic has to be weighed against the advantage of having had to learn how to design your own. The advantage of being easily pigeonholed as "a student of X's" has to be weighed against the disadvantage of being pigeonholed at all and the potential difficulty of distancing yourself from X's reputation if you need to. Mentors and student fieldworkers should be aware of the potential for exploitation as well as the potential for mutual benefit, and students should be able to choose to become part of the professor's project or to do their own.

Another set of issues is raised by the need for funding. From the beginning in the 1960s, sociolinguistic research has relied on corporate and governmental support that was made available, in part, for political reasons. One large source of funding for linguistic research in the post–World War II era was the U.S. Department of Education, acting on the mandate of the National Defense Education Act (NDEA). The NDEA was enacted in response to the perceived Soviet threat in the aftermath of Sputnik. The Center for Applied Linguistics, host to important early sociolinguistic research, was funded by the Ford Foundation.

Some sociolinguistic research projects require no more than that the researchers be drawing their regular salaries. But since sociolinguistic research usually requires some equipment, often requires some travel, and always requires time, many sociolinguists have to find extra sources of money. Some universities offer competitive grants, usually small and usually meant to fund projects that will later attract outside funding; these are sometimes available to graduate students as well as faculty members. State and national funding for sociolinguistic research, in the United States and elsewhere, is scarce, and competition for it fierce. Grant review processes, in which current and former grantees evaluate new proposals, can have the effect of discouraging research in new paradigms, and public funds are often restricted to projects that are in areas of particular practical need, such as education or mental health, or that contribute to one or another general governmental initiative (such as the U.S. National Endowment for the Humanities' 1992 Christopher Columbus Quincentenary initiative or the National Science Foundation's "Human Capital" initiative). Corporate research and development grants are another potential source of funding for sociolinguistic research. Corporations that farm out their research projects to independent linguistic contractors usually have specific questions they want answered.

Because research funds are tight, and because some researchers are under pressure from their departments and colleges to attract outside funding, it is tempting to design a project to fit the requirements of one source of money or another. University-sponsored workshops on "grantsmanship" sometimes encourage this sort of tailoring, and there is nothing wrong in principle with deciding that a governmental or corporate research initiative is interesting and worthwhile, and offering to contribute to it. It is of course dishonest, though, to pretend to be planning one project while actually planning something different, and worth remembering that a really sound research project in which the researcher is genuinely interested will be a great deal easier and more interesting to work on than a project designed to get a grant.

The Uses of Results

Why do we do research? It used to be thought that the answer to this question was simple: to discover truth, thereby advancing knowledge. Many humanists and social scientists are skeptical about this answer now. As the academy has begun to take the experiences of non-Western peoples, women, and nondominant ethnic groups more seriously, we have come to suspect there are multiple truths and multiple ways of making sense of the world, and we can see, prompted by critical theorists such as Foucault (1980), that knowledge and power are not coincidentally related: those who have or can produce knowledge can control those who do not. There have always been covert agendas for scholarly research in addition to the

nobler overt ones: scholars have always needed to get a job, to please
the King, to advance the Reformation, to meet the Ph.D. requirements, to get tenure, to feel good about themselves, and so on.

It is easy to let skepticism turn into cynicism. But admitting that
the explicit and implicit goals of scholarly research are sometimes
unclear and multiple and potentially nefarious does not require that
we abandon the possibility of scholarship. It does require that we
think about our agendas, though.

For one thing, we have to think about the questions we ask. As
most of us have noticed, questions that seem fascinating to students
sometimes turn out, in the professor's opinion, to be trivial or uninteresting, and it is more often the professor than the student whose
opinion carries the day. As I have pointed out before, what seems to
be an interesting, researchable question in one decade may have
seemed to be a trivial, uninteresting one in a previous decade, and
the ebb and flow of what questions are askable and answerable has
much to do with who is in power. This does not mean that new questions cannot be asked, and it does not mean that what seems interesting now is simply what powerful people want others to think
about. It does mean that we need to think about why we ask the questions we ask and not others.

We also have to think about who we study and how we talk about
them. Sociolinguistic research is frequently about members of relatively powerless groups: working-class speakers, inner-city African-
Americans, isolated nonindustrialized cultural groups, women, and
so on. Sociolinguists' goals in studying such people have much that
is noble about them: in addition to wanting answers to questions
about linguistic variation and change, we have always wanted to
understand and maybe help people whose ways of talking are stigmatized or silenced. But descriptions of less-powerful groups can easily be read as critiques, and deciding that someone else needs help
can easily be seen as condescending, as a way of asserting power and
control. (On a one-on-one interactional scale, this is why an offer of
help from a superior can be both appreciated and infuriating.) And
well-intentioned linguistic research sometimes disrupts and disturbs
the people it is about.

We should also be aware, as Cameron et al. (1992) point out,
that research that *studies* groups of people also has the effect of *creating* groups of people. No matter how many disclaimers are added,
labeling a linguistic variety "African-American Vernacular English"

or "Southern speech" creates a group of speakers, African-Americans or Southerners, potentially obscuring the fact that African-Americans and Southerners have many identities and many ways of talking. People do not like to be told that they act the way they do because of social facts about them, and we should take this seriously. To suggest that people's behavior is determined by their group memberships, as sociolinguists often do, is to suggest that people do not have individual voices and do not make creative, responsible choices, and thus to deny people an aspect of their humanity.

Finally, we have to think about our goals. Linguists have traditionally thought of themselves as descriptivists. For good reason, it seems important to us to distance ourselves from the prescriptive usage mavens of the newspapers and the traditional writing classes who bemoan linguistic change and insist on often arbitrary standards. So we teach our students and convince ourselves that our job is to describe without evaluating. Some sociolinguists question this attitude, though, wondering if describing is not in some ways really advocating the status quo and suggesting that sociolinguistic research be used "critically," to effect social change (Fairclough, 1985; Hodge and Kress, 1993). They wonder whether research can ever be purely descriptive and evaluatively neutral and argue that since it cannot, sociolinguists may as well be explicit about what they hope their work will accomplish in the world.

This chapter has raised many more questions than it has answered. In the end, we can never be absolutely sure that we are being completely fair to and honest with the people we study or the people who help us, or that our motives in conducting research are completely pure. We can either become paralyzed by this or we can try to make the best of it. Sociolinguists by definition do the latter, since people who are intellectually paralyzed are not doing any research, sociolinguistic or otherwise. The best we can do in planning sociolinguistic research (as in any other endeavor) is to think conscientiously about issues such as the ones raised here and decide in advance how we will deal with them.

DISCUSSION QUESTIONS

1. Find out what the procedures are at your university for getting approval for research with human subjects. Would a project in

sociolinguistics have to be approved by your institution's review board? Why or why not? Is a specific informed consent form required or suggested?

2. Here are some issues that were not touched on, or touched on only lightly, in this chapter. How would you handle each one and why?

   a. Under what circumstances is it acceptable to use students—your own or other people's—as research subjects? In what ways might the fact that potential research subjects are students complicate the process of getting true informed consent? How might students expect to be rewarded for participation in a research project?

   b. What special legal and ethical issues come up when research participants are minors? Under what circumstances do minors have actual choices about whether or not to participate in research projects at their schools, for example?

   c. Certain forms of discourse are generally considered public, part of the record which anyone can quote or refer to. These include, for example, transcripts of speeches by public officials, tapes or transcripts of public meetings of governmental organizations, and published material of most kinds (though permission to quote copyrighted material is often required). Journalists, for example, are free to examine and use public material without obtaining the consent of its authors. Sociolinguists may want to use material like this as data. What ethical issues does this raise, if any? Should we get informed consent for our uses of people's public speeches, for example, since our uses may differ from journalists' uses?

   d. Journalists also regularly interview people without getting informed consent. Sociolinguistic research also sometimes includes interviews with expert consultants, for which we do not normally need to get human-subjects permission or use consent forms. Does this raise any potential problems? What if we decide that the interviews are interesting for linguistic reasons as well as for the information we acquire through them?

e. Should you pay people for participating in your research? Under what circumstances? What other forms of compensation are there? Are there ever situations in which research participants should not be compensated?

3. Discuss how issues of power and control might be part of the hidden agenda as a student writes a thesis or dissertation and committee members comment on it and eventually accept it.

SUGGESTIONS FOR FURTHER READING

Cameron et al. (1992) provide an interesting and useful collection of essays about the connections between ethics and method in sociolinguistic research, and in Josselson (1996), narrative researchers from a variety of disciplines discuss similar issues. Lindlof (1995) includes a good discussion of informed consent and a sample consent form. Larmouth (1992) discusses surreptitious recording in sociolinguistics. Many of the chapters in Paulston and Tucker (1997) suggest ways sociolinguistic research was, from the beginning, enabled, shaped, and constrained by institutional and governmental sources of funding.

◆ 5 ◆

Standards of Evidence

HOW DO YOU KNOW WHEN YOU'RE RIGHT?

Some of us come into sociolinguistics with backgrounds in human-istic disciplines in which standards of evidence are not often dis-cussed. In essays and examinations for literature courses, for exam-ple, paying close attention to the language of the text is often a good idea; misunderstanding or not noticing a major theme is usu-ally a bad idea; a coherent theoretical perspective helps and some-times one particular theoretical perspective (New Critical, Femi-nist, or New Historical, for example) or another seems to be required. But exactly what makes one interpretation more right than another is not often explicitly discussed. This can lead to frustra-tion: apprentice literary critics can come to feel that doing good work is as much a matter of second-guessing the potential audience or successfully adapting to the professor's theoretical bias as a mat-ter of saying right things about texts. It can also lead to creativity, a kind of artistry in interpretation that is more difficult in disci-plines with more clearly defined standards of evidence.

Other sociolinguists' backgrounds are in fields such as experi-mental psychology, sociology, and educational research in which standards of evidence are very clearly delineated. In statistics and methodology courses, students learn exactly how to design their research so that others will take its results seriously and how to test their findings against relatively fixed standards for rightness or wrongness. To be significant for the purposes of many researchers, for example, research results have to be quantified—turned into

58

numbers—and then undergo statistical tests that show that the results have less than some predefined chance—less than 5% or 1%—of having occurred randomly. Patterns that do not pass tests

---

Box 5.1   Using "Random" and "Significant"

"Random" and "significant" have everyday uses which are different from their technical uses. Because more and more of the readers of sociolinguists' work are accustomed to seeing these words used in their technical senses, it is best to avoid using them in the nontechnical senses when talking about research.

Random, in its technical sense, means the result of actions that occur in a completely arbitrary order or for completely arbitrary reasons. A common example of a result that could appear non-random when it really is random is the process by which enough monkeys poking at enough keyboards for enough time would eventually produce a Shakespeare sonnet, not because the monkeys are poets but simply because the number of possible combinations of letters and spaces is not infinite. Because the non-technical use of "random" to mean "assorted" or "various" is quite informal, it does not often slip into written research reports. Be careful, however, not to use "random" in this informal way in an oral report of a research project.

A *significant* result is one that meets certain well-defined statistical criteria, determined via mathematical calculations. Significant results are ones that would have been very unlikely to occur as the result of random processes. So avoid writing or saying "there is a significant difference between the two groups" or "these results are significant because" unless you mean that you have analyzed your results statistically and can show formal statistical significance. To put it another way, avoid using "significant" as a synonym for "interesting" or "intriguing" or "surprising" or "bigger than I expected," since this may make some readers think you are making claims you may be unable to support.

of statistical significance can be called "trends" but not "results"; they can be discussed but are not taken as truths.

The requirements of quantitative research can be frustrating for student researchers who do not have the resources to produce believ-able statistical results in their own projects (not enough subjects, not enough raters, not enough trials, etc.), and a common nickname for one of the required courses in these fields is "sadistics." But it can be comforting to know exactly how to proceed with research and exactly how to argue for the rightness of one's results, and the trends found in small pilot studies can lead to important larger-scale research.

The contrast between definitions of "rightness" in the humani-ties and in the social sciences emphasizes a fact that has been the subject of considerable recent discussion: different disciplines have different "logics" and "rhetorics of inquiry" [see, for example, Nel-son et al. (1987) and Pera (1994)]. This is to say that basic start-ing assumptions, procedures for arriving at rightness, and procedures for communicating results to others all differ from discipline to dis-cipline and from discourse community to discourse community within a discipline. What counts as proof in one area may not count in another; "truth" is relative. The possibility of relativism is frus-trating for people brought up to trust the "scientific method" and can be frightening for people who believe that there are absolute moral standards for right and wrong behavior. One possible reac-tion is cynicism: if there are multiple truths and multiple ways of arriving at truth, why bother doing research?

In this chapter we explore the alternatives to cynicism. Because there are no universally agreed on methods for proving things in our field (we can give ourselves credit for realizing that there can-not be), qualitative sociolinguistic researchers cannot incontro-vertibly prove that they are right (or wrong). But we can discover and say things that are plausible, relevant to practical problems, and important for our understanding of how language and society work. As Agar (1996a, p. 13) puts it, "we're not doing Enlightenment sci-ence, but we're not working randomly, either." Or, in the formula-tion of Erikson (1986, p. 147), "Conclusive proof is often not pos-sible. . . . Yet some lines of interpretation can be shown to be more robust than others. On that admittedly shaky ground must rest the possibility of intellectual integrity and credibility in interpretive research."

Reliability and Validity in Qualitative Research

One way of evaluating the "robustness" of research techniques is in terms of their *validity* and *reliability*. A research procedure is "reliable" if it produces the same results each time it is employed. A procedure is "valid" if the results it yields are correct or true. Obviously, neither of these criteria is easy to apply in interpretive sociolinguistic research, since we work with people. Even in the most constrained situations, no two people behave the same way, no two observers are likely to take identical field notes, and no two readers come to exactly the same understanding of a text. What we mean by reliability, obtaining "the same results" on multiple tries, cannot mean precisely what it does in a tightly controlled experiment in which results are phrased in numbers. What we mean by validity is a function of what we mean by truth, and many humanists and social scientists are skeptical about the possibility of absolute truth and limit their search to knowledge that holds for certain purposes, in certain contexts, and for certain people.

Yet there are ways of approximating reliability and validity in qualitative research. To determine whether a procedure is reliable, we can try it repeatedly. We can ask lots of people the same questions, for example. We can have different people try the procedure, if that is practical, systematically asking them to look at data, asking the same questions or applying the same labeling and categorization schemes. Procedures can be tried in different settings and at different times. (For example, sociolinguists have asked people to tell "danger of death" or "most embarrassing moment" stories in many contexts, and this has often turned out to be a good way to elicit fairly fluent speech.) Sometimes, although probably not often enough, sociolinguists purposely test the reliability of each other's research techniques by making efforts to replicate their findings, doing the same thing in a different setting to see if the results are the same.

"Diversity of method" (Kirk and Miller, 1986, p. 30) is also important. Diversity of method is also sometimes known as "triangulation." It means using more than one form of evidence or more than one procedure. Listening to people talking or analyzing written texts is often our main technique, but we can also ask people about how they use language, ask others about them, look for historical and literary evidence, and so on. Each source of data requires a different sort of caution (as we know, for example, there are aspects of people's talk that they are not good at describing, and literary representations of speech are not necessarily intended to be accurate), but each provides a different sort of insight.

Ultimately, reliable procedures are the result of time and care. The more time you spend in the research "site," be it a place, a text, or a set of tapes, the more likely you are to have tried things repeatedly and in different ways. It is no accident that some of the most creative and influential work in sociolinguistics has been done by people who knew their research participants or texts intimately. To give just one example, Heath's (1983) very well-known study of modes of orality and literacy in "Roadville" and "Trackton" was the result of 10 years of living and working there. The fact that most graduate schools will not allow 10 years of dissertation data gathering is another argument for working with something you already know well.

How can we tell when a conclusion we draw is valid? From a philosophical point of view, this may be an unanswerable question. But for the practical purposes of seeing whether we can say new, useful things about language, most sociolinguists would probably agree with Rampton (1995a, p. 249) that "the relatively modest assumption that there are phenomena beyond one's own current state of consciousness is itself enough to warrant a central place for questions of validity." One question we can ask is whether we are really observing what we set out to observe. For example, a sociolinguist interested in the social correlates of rural-sounding speech might suppose that rural-sounding speakers would be found in rural areas. But "rural" may not be as straightforward a category as it once was. Defining a person who grew up in a relatively small town as rural and a person who grew up in a suburb or a city as urban ignores the fact that in some places— such as the country music industry—ruralness is as much a symbolic as a demographic category.

We can also ask whether we have labeled things in the best way. To talk about correct words for things is to assume that although signs may be arbitrary in some sense, their daily human uses are not. For practical purposes, that is, there may be better and worse words for things. For example, "author" in its everyday sense is a cover term for several different roles in the production of discourse. As Goffman pointed out (1974), "animators" who write things down may or may not be the "authors" who designed the text or the "prin-

cipals" whose commitments the words express. Using the term
"author" in Goffman's more precise way may cast light on patterns
that are obscured if we use the term in its broader sense. Another
example, which has already been alluded to, is the use of terms such
as "African-American Vernacular English," "Chicano English," or
"Mexican Spanish" to refer to linguistic varieties. Since any variety is an abstraction—there are no groups of people who all speak
exactly the same way all the time—labeling a variety creates an
artificial group and implies that a shared way of speaking characterizes everyone in the group all the time. Yet we need to have ways
of referring to the generalizations we make about ways of talking
and ways of identifying oneself. So we have to think carefully about
the terms we choose and their implications, and some terms are better than others.

Furthermore, we can ask whether we really know what the variables are. For a long time, for example, sociolinguists have noted
that gender is correlated with linguistic variation. But for most of
this time we have assumed that gender was dichotomous and a function of biological sex—people were either (always and completely)
female or (always and completely) male—and that sexuality and
gender always matched. This obscured the ways in which gender
could be continuous and changeable and ignored the independent
variable of sexual orientation (see Eckert and McConnell-Ginet,
1992; Bing and Bergvall, 1996). We risk making a similar validity
error in assuming that "style" is simply a matter of how much attention a speaker is paying to his or her speech, by assuming that social
class is always relevant, by assuming that a particular word in a text
is either a noun or a verb, not both, or by failing to realize that the
fit of a person's false teeth can affect the sibilance of his /s/'s. Since
observations are always "theory dependent" (see Chapter 3), we
have to scrutinize the explicit and unconscious theories we start out
with very carefully.

No adequate results can emerge from inadequate evidence. Erikson (1986, p. 140) suggests that there are five major types of "evidentiary inadequacy":

1. inadequate amounts of evidence
2. inadequate variety in kinds of evidence
3. faulty interpretive status of evidence (that is, the researcher
   misunderstands what is happening or what it means)

4. inadequate disconfirming evidence (the researcher does not
have data that might disconfirm his or her assertions, or does
not have evidence that such data were systematically sought)
5. inadequate discrepant case analysis (in other words, not
enough attention has been paid to apparent exceptions; we
discuss how to be systematic about this below)

Researchers are almost inevitably biased in favor of results they
expect or hope for, so, as mechanical as they may seem, heuristics
such as Erikson's for evaluating evidence are important. In the end,
though, reliability and validity really involve having enough good
evidence and examining it repeatedly and thoroughly, with a critical eye on one's own assumptions.

Evaluating Competing Interpretations

Even if we do everything we can to make our procedures reliable
and ensure that our interpretations of their results are valid, it is
still likely that our interpretation will not be the only possible one.
A large part of the research process is deciding which of two or more
ways of explaining a pattern is the best and arguing for that explanation. The proposal and evaluation of competing interpretations
are part of the process of thought and writing that goes into a
research report and, if the work is taken seriously, a part of the
process of scholarly discussion and disputation that follows it. Thus
is it is important to make systematic efforts to generate "rival
hypotheses" and to take such competing interpretations seriously
from the beginning. "Negative case analysis" (Lindlof, 1995, p. 240)
is one way to do this. This involves no more than making explicit
and conscious the process by which hypotheses are usually created
and refined. After a hypothesis is developed, the researcher keeps
testing it with new data, revising it if necessary, until no more cases
can be found that are not accounted for. In the process of asking
systematically whether each particular observation fits, the initial
generalization gets refined, or it topples under the weight of adjust-
ments and caveats and a new generalization takes its place.

　　Competing interpretations are often the result of differences in
point of view. For example, is the increasingly common spelling of
the contraction of *it is* as *its* an example of incorrectness due to igno-

rance and carelessness? Is it an example of orthographic change in progress driven in part by internal analogy (the spelling of the possessive *its*)? Or is it a performance error, simply a slip of the pen or fingers? The answer depends on whether you ask an English teacher, a linguist, or someone who is neither. It depends on the English teacher's politics and training. It depends on whether the linguist is answering questions on a grammar hot line, teaching teachers-to-be, or writing about linguistic change. The person who writes *its* for *it is* might have made an embarrassing mistake or might be making a small gesture of resistance; or it might be meaningless, just something that does not matter. Which explanation is right? It depends on why the question is asked and for whose purposes. There is no way of deciding out of context.

Realizing this, sociolinguists and other interpretive researchers have proposed ways of making sure they elicit a variety of points of view. One way is referred to as "member checking," "feedback," or "playback." Member checking involves asking the people you are studying whether your analysis of their behavior is right. In playback or feedback procedures, as mentioned earlier, recordings of participants' speech are played to them and the participants comment on what was happening and why. Here is how Tannen (1984, p. 39) describes playback sessions in her research on "conversational style" in dinner-table talk:

> Playback was a sensitive process. Because this was the way that the other members of the group showed me the interaction from their perspectives, it was important for them to direct the session. I had to be careful to wait for them to make comments and not put ideas in their heads or words in their mouths. Therefore, I gave them control of the tape recorder. They could stop it and comment when they liked, and they could start it again when they felt they were finished commenting. In the event, however, that an episode I had singled out for analysis or another participant had commented upon was not the subject of comment by another participant, I did then call attention to the segment. In those cases I began with the most general questions and only as a last resort made specific mention of what I thought might be going on or what another had observed. The playback sessions were recorded for later reference, and to obviate the need to take notes, which might have hampered the spontaneity of comments.

Research subjects are biased, of course—people want to sound some ways and not others and to be credited with some motivations and not others—and this has to be taken into account. Although it is tempting, particularly with people you like and respect, simply to let them give their own account of their sociolinguistic behavior, most sociolinguists aim for composite explanations that take into account the points of view of participants and nonparticipants, insiders and outsiders, linguist and research participants, giving no single set of interests the exclusive right to provide the explanation. Involving the people being studied in the research is not just ethically sound (see Chapter 4) but intellectually wise.

There are also more subjective ways of evaluating interpretations. In field research, just as in a library literature search, you eventually reach a point at which you seem to be finding out the same things over and over again. Eventually you find that you stop being surprised by what participants do, that new data are not adding much to your understanding of the situation or the process you are studying, and that you feel confident that you understand what is going on (Lindlof, 1995, pp. 241–242). At this point there will still be things you do not know or do not completely understand, but they can be separated and saved for another paper or another project. It is perfectly possible to feel confident about the wrong answer to a question, of course, but, in conjunction with other evidence, confidence can be a helpful clue. For many newcomers to interpretive research, deciding when a stopping point has been reached is one of the most difficult things to do.

Even after taking all these precautions, you can never be sure that your interpretation is the only possible one or even the best one. Thus it is particularly important in qualitative research to be able to state your evidence for every claim you make. Erikson (1986) calls this statement of evidence for a claim an "evidentiary warrant," and suggests that evidentiary warrants be developed by "reviewing the data corpus repeatedly to test the validity of the assertions that were generated, seeking disconfirming evidence as well as confirming evidence" (p. 146). In other words, once again, study your data systematically and repeatedly.

In addition, it is important to be clear about the reasons your interpretation may differ from others. Be reflexive: be aware of and able to discuss your own role in the research and in its results. No matter how cleverly a project is designed, the researcher almost inevitably has some effect on what happens in the situation being studied. People know (as they have to; see Chapter 4) that they are being recorded or observed, and their answers to questions about what they do are inevitably influenced by their guesses about what the researcher thinks they should do. Researchers' experiences with previous texts affect their experiences with new ones, and we are all better at discovering interesting intricacy in things we like than in things we do not like.

It is also important to be clear about how generalizable your findings are. Since we rarely use random samples of speakers or linguistic items and do not have standardized criteria for generating representative samples, we are usually working with small and possibly idiosyncratic populations or data sets. It is tempting to claim that your findings are more generally true than you can show they are—that the behavior of the middle-class people in one city shows what Midwesterners do, that the interactions of one psychotherapist with his or her clients show how psychotherapists in general interact with clients in general, or that the behavior of a few women in a few hours of conversation shows how women talk. Although we of course want our findings to be useful and enlightening outside of the immediate research setting, we can only suggest that they might be, and let others find out for sure by studying other people. Conversely, if a claim *is* general—if there is reason to believe a feature or a pattern is universal, or at least applicable beyond your research site—this needs to be made clear and argued for. If you think that silence is appropriate when getting to know someone not only for Athabaskans but for all Native Americans, if you think that there are psychological or sociobiological reasons why women should be more community oriented and men more contest minded, or if it seems likely that interactions between psychotherapists and their clients *have* to work a certain way because of the demands of the situation or that talk to nonintimates is *necessarily* more explicit than talk to intimates, then be clear about this.

Be aware of and discuss the issue of replicability, too. If someone else were to repeat your study, would he or she come to the same conclusions? Would it even be possible for your study to be replicated? The more thoroughly you discuss your biases, assumptions, and research procedures, the more likely it is that someone else, doing the same thing, would find similar results (Cresswell, 1974, p. 159). Although it is rare for sociolinguists to replicate the studies of others formally, we commonly get ideas from one another about what sorts of groups or linguistic phenomena to study and how to proceed. It should not be a mystery, then, exactly how the data were collected, by whom, and under what circumstances; how the analysis was carried out (if only just "by looking repeatedly for patterns"); how the researcher decided on the research site and what his or her background was there; and what his or her previous relationship to participants was. If you are the mother or teacher or friend of the people you are studying, for example, say so. It is frustrating to read a paper or a thesis that gives the technical specifications of the tape recorder the researcher used, when any tape recorder would presumably have recorded the same data, but fails to say how the researcher decided what to record.

This brings us to a final point, to which we return later in the book: beware of scientistic-sounding rhetoric. Language that makes it sound as if procedures are more replicable than they are (such as giving the specifications of your equipment when it does not really make any difference what equipment another researcher might use) or results more generalizable than they are (such as saying "people do x" when what you really mean is "the people I studied did x in this situation") is misleading—and annoying for readers.

Summary

This chapter has discussed issues that have to do with how claims are supported and what constitutes compelling evidence. Different research traditions have different standards for evaluating evidence. Standards of evidence for qualitative research about human beings are difficult to define but important to consider. Evidence for a claim has to be assembled in such a way that the same procedure would yield similar results if carried out again (this is referred to as "reliability"), and the evidence has to be accurate and relevant (this is referred to as "validity"). In a variety of ways, researchers can try to ensure that the evidence they assemble is as reliable and valid as possible and that their interpretation of it has been scrutinized as closely as possible. In the end, no matter how good their evidence, qualitative sociolinguists must be careful not to make unwarranted generalizations, on purpose or even by mistake.

DISCUSSION QUESTIONS

1. [Note: This is a good discussion project to do before you read this chapter.] Here is a list of standards of rightness. What does "right" seem to mean in each case? In what contexts does each get used? Which of these have you used in evaluating things you read or heard? Which do you think should be used? Which are more and less desirable? Are any completely inappropriate in all situations or completely appropriate in all situations?

   a. If somebody powerful said it, it's right; if somebody powerless said it, it's probably wrong.
   b. If others can be persuaded of a claim, then it's right.
   c. If a claim is consistent with what it says in the Bible (or some other authoritative source), then it's right. (This, for example, would be an argument for creationism over the theory of evolution.)
   d. If a claim is true it's right.
   e. An essay that is well written is more likely to be right than one that isn't.
   f. If a claim has less than a 5% chance of being wrong, then it should be considered right.
   g. If you believe it, it's right.
   h. If the analysis satisfies certain preset requirements, then the claim is right. (For example, formal theories of language are supposed to be descriptively adequate, explanatorily adequate, and economical. In physics, theories are supposed to be elegant in certain ways.)
   i. If the argumentation satisfies certain preset requirements, then the claim is right. (This is the standard for formal, syllogistic logic.)
   j. If a claim is objective, then it's right.
   k. If a claim is potentially useful, then it's right.
   l. If it's in print it's probably right.
   m. A claim that doesn't make too large a leap away from what is currently accepted in the profession is more likely to be right than one that does.
   n. An explanation that accounts for all aspects of the data is more likely to be right than one that accounts for only part of the data.

o. You can't possibly be "right," so just say whatever you want.

2. Here is how Deborah Tannen (1984, p. 38) describes what she calls "the aha factor," one of several ways she evaluates the rightness of her analyses of conversation.

> If my interpretation is correct, then readers, on hearing my explication, will exclaim within their heads, "Aha!" Something they have intuitively sensed will have been made explicit. Most discovery, ultimately, is a process of explaining the known. When the subject of analysis is human interaction—a process that we all engage in, all our lives—each reader can measure interpretation against her/his own experience. If an interpretation is misguided, no large number of readers will be deeply impressed by it; it will fade. If it is true, or has grasped a portion of the truth, it will be remembered.

Argue for and/or against the aha factor as a standard of evidence.

SUGGESTIONS FOR FURTHER READING

More detailed discussions of validity and reliability in qualitative social-science research are Kirk and Miller (1986) and Altheide and Johnson (1994). See also Lindlof (1995, pp. 238–242). Erikson (1986) provides many practical suggestions (some borrowed here) for how to reduce the possibility of bias in data collection and analysis.

◆ 6 ◆

Thinking

INTROSPECTION AND INTUITION

It may seem odd in a book about sociolinguistic research to find introspection and intuition mentioned. Querying our own knowledge about language through examination of our own mental processes is not an acknowledged research technique in sociolinguistics. Nor are intuition or the accessing of intuition through introspection dealt with in most treatments of qualitative research in other disciplines. Yet sociolinguists do make use of their own senses of what things mean, of the structure of words, sentences, or speech events, and of the effects of talk and how the effects are created. We do this both as we plan research and in the course of carrying it out. So it is wise to think about what linguistic and sociolinguistic intuition is, about whether and how intuitions can be accessed via introspection, and about what the uses of intuition and introspection should and should not be.

What Is Intuition? What Is Introspection?

In philosophy, "intuition" has had many meanings. It has sometimes been defined as the direct, nonempirical knowledge of nonsensory truth: humans intuit God, for example. Alternatively, intuition can mean nonempirical knowledge of empirical truth, as it did for Jung, for whom all humans shared unconscious knowledge about the world, expressed in archetypes found universally in myth. Intuition can

71

mean arriving at logical conclusions without conscious formulation of the premises on which the reasoning is based, or it can be seen as a step that follows rational thought. [See Wild (1983) for an overview of these and many other definitions of intuition in philosophy.]

Psychologists who study intuition also define the term in various ways (Westcott, 1994). Intuition has often been seen as a kind of unconscious reasoning: people make intuitive judgments without knowing what their reasons are or without being able to put their reasons into words. Intuitions may be the result of relatively idiosyncratic processes of thought rather than universal logical principles, although some believe that intuition is a component of all thinking. Alternatively, intuition is sometimes seen in psychology as independent of reason, a holistic way of apprehending the world that is aesthetic, empathetic, quick, and subjectively certain.

In Chomskyan linguistics, "intuition" is a technical term that is considerably narrower in scope. Speakers are said to "have" intuitions about two things: whether or not sentences in their language are well formed and what the structural relationships of sentences to other sentences are. This means, according to a Chomskyan, that any native speaker of English can make the judgment, without having recourse to consciously learned rules or processes of reasoning, that a sentence such as

I thought that Mary was ill, but it turned out that she wasn't.

is possible in English, whereas a sentence such as

I realized that Mary was ill, but it turned out that she wasn't.

sounds strange (examples from Radford, 1988, p. 5), or that the sentence

Flying planes can be dangerous.

can have either one of two meanings depending on how its structure is interpreted. Since intuitions of this sort are defined as a crucial part of the data for which generative linguistics has had to account (especially in its earlier, less abstract formulations), their use has survived challenges such as that of Labov and Baltin (Labov, 1972b, pp. 193–199), who showed that speakers' intuitions about the structure of sentences could be changed by putting the sentences into different contexts, or that of Ross (1979), who showed that no two people in a group of 29 made exactly the same set of syntactic judgments about a set of English constructions. Neither earlier formulations of generative theory, which aimed at modeling the competence of an "idealized" (completely competent) speaker in a homogeneous speech community, nor more recent versions, which aim at modeling the universal mental structures that underlie any human's ability to use language, require attention to contextual aspects of meaning or to the variations among actual speakers, so critiques such as these are in fact somewhat irrelevant.

Introspection, or looking inward, is a technique of psychological research. It involves training people to report their sensory experiences and thought processes in detail. The technique is used, for example, in the "talk-aloud protocols" which have been used to study the cognitive processes involved in skills such as writing (e.g., Flower et al., 1990). Although the term "introspection" is not used in generative linguistics, the examination of our own mental states and processes is the source of linguistic intuitions.

Introspective Research in Sociolinguistics: An Example

Among the influential early sociolinguists were people whose training and research backgrounds were in generative linguistics. Not surprisingly, they brought the introspective research techniques they were familiar with into the study of language and society. One such scholar, whose influence inaugurated an important sociolinguistic subfield, was Robin Lakoff, whose *Language and Woman's Place* was published in 1975. Lakoff's research for this book was based on introspection and very informal observation. As she put it, "The data on which I am basing my claims have been gathered mainly by introspection: I have examined my own speech and that of my acquaintances, and have used my own intuitions in analyzing it" (p. 4).

Lakoff defends her methodology on several grounds. In anticipation of criticism of the source of her data, she points out that "*any* procedure is at some point introspective: the gatherer must analyze his data, after all" (p. 5). In anticipation of criticism of her research population (herself and her acquaintances), she points out that "one necessarily selects a subgroup of the population to work with: is the educated, white, middle-class group . . . less worthy of study than any other?" Lakoff argues that although "this study does in itself represent the speech of only a small subpart of the community, it is still of use in indicating directions for further research in this area: in providing a basis for comparison, a taking-off point for further studies" (p. 5). Anticipating criticism of the representativeness of her data, she points out that collecting enough relevant data through more "random" procedures would take a lot of time and good luck; "if we are to have a good sample of data to analyze, this will have to be elicited artificially from someone; I submit I am as good an artificial source of data as anyone" (p. 5).

Lakoff's work has been criticized in precisely the ways she expected (sometimes by people who seem not to know that she was aware of the possibility). In the first place, subsequent language-and-gender scholars have asked, what is the status of introspection and intuition in sociolinguistics? Strictly speaking, the researcher's linguistic intuitions are methodologically useful only if it can be assumed that the researcher's senses of linguistic appropriateness and structure are the same as other people's. In other words, intuitions can be taken as valid only if it is assumed that the researcher is either an example of the idealized speaker–hearer whose linguistic competence generative syntacticians describe or a typical member of the homogeneous speech community whose norms for speech many sociolinguists describe. Lakoff was describing not only linguistic competence, but also language attitudes and how language use could evoke and express attitudes, and she was quite specifically describing the competences and attitudes of a heterogeneous group consisting of women and men, so neither criterion for the use of intuition applies.

In the second place, others have asked, to what extent can well-educated middle-class white women be taken as representative of women in general? Although Lakoff did not claim that her research sample represented anything except a small subset of women, it is easy to interpret her book (as well as much subsequent language-and-gender writing) as making larger generalizations than are warranted. This has to do with the way observations are phrased. When a person writes "there is at least one rule that a woman [rather than "the women I studied"] will use more in conversation than a man" (Lakoff, 1975, p. 14) or "it is important for women friends [rather than "these women friends"] to avoid expressing themselves in a hard-and-fast way" (Coates, 1996, p. 167), she is suggesting through grammatical choices that her claims apply universally, to all women and all men. The issue of "the grammar of particularity"—how to keep claims from sounding more general than they are meant to be—is discussed in more detail in Chapter 9. The point to bear in mind is that misleading generalizations that are taken as fact create models of language and society that are biased by ethnocentricity (everyone is like us) or provinciality (everything is the way it is here).

The third critique Lakoff anticipated had to do with whether her data—assorted things she heard around her and in the media, together with her own intuitions—were in fact representative of the speech and beliefs of the people she was explicitly studying. It is not so much the "randomness" of the data that is in question. Although tried early in sociolinguistics, notably by Labov (1966), random techniques for selecting subjects or eliciting speech are now rarely used. Instead, the issue is the systematicity of data collection and analysis. Ethnographers, for example, spend months or years in their research sites, listening, taping, making notes, asking questions, and trying out hypotheses (see Chapter 7). Discourse analysts, though they tend to work with much smaller amounts of data, benefit from careful thought about exactly what texts to use and heuristic techniques to make sure they have thought about the texts systematically (see Chapter 8). And researchers who elicit data "artificially" do so by asking not one but many carefully chosen speakers.

Despite all this, *Language and Women's Place* has had exactly the effect Lakoff hoped for, sparking over two decades of research about language and gender. Not surprisingly, the generalizations Lakoff made have not turned out to be true everywhere and for everyone, and her unstated models of language and society as fairly static entities that exist before and outside of interaction have been challenged. But Lakoff's intuitive, introspective study has, without a doubt, been very important, and her research techniques cannot simply be dismissed. So let us think more about the roles intuition can play in sociolinguistic research.

Roles for Intuition in Sociolinguistics?

To discuss the roles intuition can (and inevitably does) play in sociolinguistic research, we need to distinguish two kinds of intuition.

The first is intuition in the Chomskyan sense: direct access to our own linguistic competence via introspection. The second is intuition as informal, unsystematic, unconscious reasoning: the sense that you know what is going on without being able to say exactly how you know. Both kinds of intuition can be useful in sociolinguistics, if they are analyzed carefully.

Intuitions About Competence. Sociolinguists have shown over and over that people's intuitions about their own language use are unreliable. Most people would have no idea how to answer some of the questions sociolinguists ask, or even what the questions mean ("How often do you vocalize /l/, and in what contexts?"). When speakers are asked more generally about "better"-sounding and "worse"-sounding pronunciations, they misreport their own usage. (This was shown, for example, in Trudgill's well-known 1972 study, in which he found that Norwich women said they used prestige variants more often than they actually did, and Norwich men said they used stigmatized variants more often than they actually did.) Sociolinguists reporting on the details of their own pronunciation and grammar would probably not be much more accurate than laypeople are.

Still, there are levels on which some people do, sometimes, know what they are doing with language. Speakers of stigmatized varieties, such as Southern American English, are typically more aware of the strategic power of language than are speakers of more prestigious varieties that seem neutral and transparent. In my work in Texas, for example (Johnstone and Bean, 1997), I found that the public language users I am studying can sometimes talk very perceptively about the linguistic choices they make. By the same token, some sociolinguists may sometimes get what they do exactly right just by thinking about it, and they can find out whether their intuitions are accurate through empirical research.

Sociolinguists' intuitions about their own speech may, in other words, sometimes be a useful first step, a way of arriving at hypotheses that can then be tested. Intuitions about our speech are of course especially useful in studying ourselves or people like us. The ability cautiously to use intuitions in this way is one argument, in fact, for studying people like yourself, the way Lakoff, Deborah Tannen (1981), and Livia Polanyi (1985), among many others, have.

But what of the role of intuitions about your own knowledge of language in studying the speech of people who are not like you? Here even more caution is needed. It is inevitable that people's perceptions of what is happening in an unfamiliar setting or situation are affected by the expectations they have formed based on familiar settings and situations. There is no other way to think about new things. But since we know that people's own understandings of what they do with talk—the meanings people attach to linguistic choices—vary widely from group to group and sometimes even from individual to individual, we need to exercise continual care in forming our initial hypotheses and continually critique our inevitable tendency to use our own intuitions and thus to attribute our own meanings to others' words and actions.

Intuitive Leaps. The role of cognitive leaps in all the sciences is well documented. A pattern suddenly and surprisingly emerges from a mass of data, an explanation seems to suggest itself, and in a flash we realize what has been going on all along. Intuitive leaps are probably not as mysterious as they seem. Although flashes of intuition are sometimes attributed to external causes (God, for example, or some sort of irrational feminine principle), their actual workings are probably fairly well captured by the classic lightbulb-goes-on-in-the-head image. The intuitive flash occurs when mental circuits get completed in normal ways, as a result of rational processes of deduction, induction, and analogical "abduction." A solution that works understandably seems more dramatic, more like a flash, than all the mental circuit-completion attempts that did not work along the way.

Intuitions of this sort are an inevitable aspect of sociolinguistic hypothesis formation. We form hypotheses by seeing things happen a certain way often enough that we induce that, for some reason, they may always happen that way or by reading about how things work in one sociolinguistic setting or process and, by analogy, making a leap to another setting or process, wondering whether things work the same way there. We are not always aware, at first, of exactly how we arrive at the questions we start with, exactly what made our topics seem interesting.

One way or another, intuitions like these have to become explicit. This often occurs in the process of writing the initial proposal or abstract of a research project—and for this reason it can be very useful to write out plans in advance, even if not required to do so by a teacher, a granting agency, or a graduate committee. Writing necessitates elaboration, and it is often in the process of completing the sentence "This project is of potential interest because" that we analyze the intuitions that gave rise to it.

Intuitive leaps are also part of the process of analysis. As sociolinguists read through their field notes, watch or audit their recordings over and over again, or tabulate the answers to their questions, patterns or explanations can emerge in intuitive flashes. Conclusions arrived at in this way can be useful, but only if the process by which they came to be is made explicit. Making analytical leaps explicit requires the discipline of systematicity, a theme to which we return in subsequent chapters. Broadly speaking, systematicity in analysis means starting with a list of questions to ask or things to look for and making sure you have asked all the questions or examined all the possibilities on your list before deciding that the analysis is complete. "Having the feeling" that you understand what is going on in your data can be useful, but only if you can then describe exactly what gave you the "feeling" and how, turning the feeling into the result of systematic observation.

DISCUSSION QUESTIONS

1. Are the following sentences acceptable in English or not? Compare your syntactic intuitions with those of other people, then discuss the usefulness of this data-collection technique. (Examples are from Radford, 1988.)

   a. My goldfish tried to escape.
   b. Your kettle is trying to boil over.
   c. My theory is trying to be foolproof.
   d. He is someone that I don't know what Mary said to.
   e. She is not a person that you can rely on.
   f. John came to see me who you met last week.
   g. Someone came to see me who said he was from the bank.
   h. Pandas live entirely off bamboo shoots.
   i. Bad weather kills entirely off bamboo shoots.

2. Do you have intuitions about the answers to any of the following questions? Compare them with those of other people. Would any of your intuitions make a good starting hypothesis for research? Under what conditions? What would be the danger involved, if any? Think also about how the questions are framed. Could you reframe any of them in ways that might result in different intuitions?

  a. Do men or women interrupt more in conversation?
  b. Are Native Americans more silent than European Americans?
  c. Is text on the World Wide Web more complex or less complex than text in books?
  d. Are Texans who identify strongly with the state of Texas more likely than others to monophthongize the /ai/ in words such as *right* and *night*?
  e. When white California high-school girls use African-American-sounding English, are they trying to identify with African-Americans?
  f. When graduate-student teaching assistants tell one another stories about amazing excuses provided by their students for late assignments, what are they accomplishing?

3. In the workbook for an introductory linguistics text, find a phonology or morphology problem you have not solved. As you solve it, pay attention to your mental processes. Are any intuitive leaps involved? At what stages?

◆ 7 ◆

Looking

PARTICIPANT OBSERVATION

A great deal of qualitative research in sociolinguistics makes use of both ethnography and discourse analysis. Ethnography is the study of culture. Discourse analysis is the study of language use. It is possible to study culture without studying discourse, but since discourse is the primary way in which culture is circulated, many anthropologists (and, by definition, all linguistic anthropologists) study language. It is also possible to study texts without studying culture; for example, Conversation Analysis is based on the belief that people create the knowledge they need to interpret the world in the process of interaction, so that there is no need to posit, or to study, any kinds of context other than the immediate context of the interaction at hand. But many sociolinguists believe that speakers do bring previously formed expectations, beliefs, and norms to bear in interaction with others, so they necessarily embed analyses of discourse in analyses of aspects of culture. In this chapter and the next we examine the field and analytical methodologies associated with ethnography and discourse analysis. Because the methods of ethnography are typically used in studying the wider contexts that give rise to discourse, we deal with it first.

The participant observation methods of ethnography have long been important in qualitative sociolinguistic work, and they are being used more and more explicitly in quantitative studies as well. A great deal has been written about how to do participant observation (see the Suggestions for Further Reading at the end of this chapter) and it is neither possible nor necessary to summarize all this material here. What I will do instead in this chapter is to provide enough of an introduction so that readers will know what participant observation is and can begin to focus an ethnographic eye on sociolinguistic phenomena. Anyone who then decides to launch a larger ethnographic project will have more reading to do, but should, after reading this chapter, know where to look.

What Is Participant Observation?
What Is Ethnography?

Participant observation is the primary research technique of ethnography, or the description of cultures. It was developed by cultural anthropologists interested in finding out from the perspective of natives what foreign cultures were like, particularly the small, isolated, traditional societies that have been the focus of anthropological research until fairly recently. Stocking (1983, p. 7) describes the main features of traditional participant observation research this way: "Entering as a stranger into a small and culturally alien community, the investigator becomes for a time and in a way part of its system of face-to-face relationships, so that the data collected in some sense reflect the native's own point of view." The experience of participant observation fieldwork is a key element of anthropology's disciplinary self-image, because such fieldwork is valued as an important formative experience for new scholars as well as because it reflects and encourages a holistic approach to describing culture and an egalitarian, relativistic ethic with respect to evaluating societies (Stocking, 1983, p. 8).

Beginning in the 1960s, anthropologists began to question the assumptions underlying participant observation, in part because worldwide decolonization began to make clear how deeply the approach was influenced by imperialistic attitudes about the relationships between "natives" and Western scholars. As a result, ethnographers began increasingly to talk about fieldwork and try out new ways of imagining whether and how participant observation can lead to knowledge. At the same time, scholars in other fields began to adopt the research methods of participant observation and join in the discussion about how to use the results.

What differentiates participant observation from casual looking around has to do with the nature of the researcher's participation in the group being studied and the care and systematicity with which records are made and analysis undertaken. Participant observers spend time developing roles for themselves in the groups in which they are interested, and then more time as group members, filling one or more roles as insiders and simultaneously making systematic efforts to come to understand what is going on in the group from the perspective of other group members. Participant observers try to uncover and record the unspoken common sense of the group they are studying, the "*immediate and local meanings*" (Erikson, 1986, p. 119) in terms of which the local world hangs together for local people.

Ethnography is based on the premise that what is distinctive about humans is our tendency to see things—objects, people, events—as having meanings. Thus an adequate description of human behavior (including linguistic behavior) has to incorporate the ways in which behavior can be interpretable as meaningful action. To use an example adapted from Erikson (1986, pp. 126–128), a person whose *behavior* could be described as "standing upright" might be seen as performing one of a variety of *actions:* "forming a line," "waiting for someone," or "giving up his or her seat on the bus." Or, to use a linguistic example, a Panamanian Kuna whose verbal behavior—the uttering of a stream of sound—could be analyzed spectrographically might be performing any one of a variety of actions: he might be speaking intelligibly or unintelligibly, in Kuna or in Spanish, having a conversation, giving a speech, uttering ritual responses to a fellow chief's speech, acting as a curer and chanting to wooden stick dolls in a special elaborated variety of Kuna, and so on (Sherzer, 1983). As we all know from experience as friends and family members, a situation does not have to be objectively real in order to be experienced as meaningful and have real human consequences: whatever you actually felt, and whether or not your blood pressure and adrenaline levels actually rose, if a loved one interprets your behavior as an expression of anger you have a real problem. Different people's relationships to the world are mediated by different traditions of and strategies for assigning meaning to things, and ethnographers are interested in learning what objects, people, and events mean for people in different situations, roles, groups, or societies. The only way to do this is to try to come to interpret the world and act in it the way locals do. Ethnographers make inferences about this tacit "local knowledge" (Geertz, 1983) based on what people say and on what people do, as well as on the artifacts they produce.

This means that one advantage of ethnography over other ways of studying humans is that ethnography provides explanations of human behavior that cannot be uncovered through other kinds of research such as experimentation, explanations that have to do with how behavior counts as action. No amount of counting of tag questions, for example, or describing their syntactic environments, could uncover how such questions are related to the expression of uncertainty, to the demands of a gender-specific identity, or to the adoption of register or generic conventions. Thus, as Spradley points out (1980, pp. 13–20), ethnography is a corrective to social theory that assumes that everyone's beliefs and behaviors can be explained in the same terms, showing instead how social theory has to be "grounded" (Glaser and Strauss 1967) in particular situations.

According to Agar (1996b, pp. 119–127), ethnography is distinguished from other approaches to social science in these ways:

- An ethnographer starts out as a learner, in a "one down" position vis-à-vis other people in the group.
- An ethnographer's research questions arise in the process of participant observation, as do hypotheses about their answers.
- The relationships an ethnographer has to develop with other people in the group under study are "long-term and diffuse" (p. 120), so the process takes time.
- An ethnographer goes to the research subjects' home turf.
- An ethnographer's descriptive assumption is holistic: all phenomena are assumed to be interconnected.

As Rampton points out (1992, pp. 56–57), because of its location and duration and the ways ethnographers have to rely on the people they study, ethnography has the potential to empower members of the researched group in ways other approaches may not. Ethnographers have to depend, at least in part, on what they are told by the people they study; they cannot just observe them or manipulate their behavior.

Ethnography in Sociolinguistics

In the earliest days of ethnography, anthropologists undertook years and years of fieldwork and then set out to describe whole cultures.

For various good reasons, contemporary ethnography tends to be less comprehensive, more oriented to the exploration of specific topics or the testing of particular hypotheses (Hymes, 1978). One of the areas on which ethnographers have focused many "microethnographies" (Spradley, 1980) is language use. The "ethnography of speaking" (or "ethnography of communication"), as this area of specialization is called, was proposed by Dell Hymes (1972, 1974; Gumperz and Hymes, 1972). Beginning in the 1960s, Hymes began to point out that a community's talk and writing were not just a way of finding out about the community's culture, but were themselves an aspect of culture worthy of study. Language use and beliefs and attitudes about language were organized and evaluated according to cultural norms in the same way as were traditionally studied aspects of culture such as religion and kinship. We will return shortly to some of Hymes' suggestions about how language use could be systematically studied by an ethnographer.

The ethnography of communication gained favor as a branch of linguistic anthropology and folklore during the 1970s, in part through the publication of an important anthology of articles edited by Bauman and Sherzer (1974, reprinted in 1989). Ethnography has always, implicitly or explicitly, been involved in sociolinguistic work in the Labovian quantitative paradigm, and quantitative sociolinguists have begun to make more explicit use of ethnographic techniques in "site studies" (Bailey, 1993; Cukor-Avila, 1996) that involve recording and analyzing all sorts of talk that go on at a research site rather than basing results exclusively on interviews with individual speakers. Although many sociolinguists believe that the "best" data come from actual recorded speech, knowledge about the cultural world in which speech is embedded is almost inevitably part of the knowledge sociolinguists bring to the analysis of these data. Explicitly or not, in other words, ethnographic observations are part of the methodology of sociolinguistics, and it can be argued that being explicit about our ethnographic methods and our reliance on their results is better than not being explicit.

Doing Ethnography: Some Preliminary Issues

Typically, ethnographers study groups of people. When groups are small, isolated, and homogeneous, they are easy to identify. A "traditional culture" may have the name of a language associated with it, and the set of users of the language may be the same as the set of people who live together and share other customs and beliefs. But although this sort of situation, in which a "speech community" is coextensive with a "culture," has long been seen as the default situation, it is in fact rare and becoming rarer. Pratt (1987) suggests, in fact, that the concept of a speech community, a cohesive, unified, conflict-free social unit, always was utopian. Most people in the world have linguistic repertoires that include resources from multiple languages and/or varieties; many people move from place to place and participate in a variety of groups, defined in a variety of ways. Boundaries that once seemed clear no longer do (Urciuoli, 1995). As Agar (1996b, pp. 6–7) puts it, "[the 'new ethnography'] views the local group as a diverse crowd in a world of blurred edges." So it is increasingly important for ethnographers of communication to think carefully about the nature of the "natural group" (Erikson, 1986, p. 128) they plan to study.

Linguists have a long tradition of dividing people into groups defined by the names of languages—Arabic speakers, Chinese speakers, English–Spanish bilinguals—and assuming that these groups are natural ones. But although there are indeed reasons for which people sometimes organize themselves into groups defined by language (as, for example, when they are trying to impose their language on others or assert their separateness from another group associated with a language), these groups are not necessarily the ones our traditional labels for languages might lead us to expect. For example, many people in Texas who would be unquestioningly identified by linguists as "Spanish–English bilinguals" themselves deny that they speak Spanish, since "Spanish" for them means standard, written Castilian or Mexican Spanish. "Spanish," in their sense, is not part of what is involved in "speaking mixed" or "Tex-Mex."

Dialectologists have of course known since the nineteenth century that boundaries between varieties are hard to draw (Chambers and Trudgill, 1980, pp. 103–124), and, whether defined by isoglosses, frequencies, or some other way, the lines we draw may not be the ones that are meaningful for people who live near them. Three speakers, all of whom can be heard to pronounce the vowel sound in "tile" as a monophthong [a], may have three different relationships to the Southern varieties of American English with which dialectologists identify this pronunciation. One (the one traditional dialectology describes best) might be from rural Georgia and use this form because, as a Southerner, it is the one he or she has always heard. One might be a Texan, for whom the monophthongal pronunciation is an expression of Texas identity (Bailey, 1991) and to whom its Southernness is incidental. To the third, from western Pennsylvania, the form might not sound Southern but simply local, a feature of "Pittsburghese."

The same set of problems arises in attempts to delineate "discourse communities," groups of people defined not by a common language but by a common communicative purpose (Killingsworth, 1996; Swales, 1990, pp. 21–32). The idea of a "community of scholars" who all use "academic English" in realizing their common goals, or of a community of politicians, landowners, and activists arguing about resource use in various sorts of "ecospeak" (Killingsworth and Palmer, 1992) is appealing and has proved useful, but in what senses are such groups "natural" ones? Most people belong to many discourse communities; they would identify themselves with some (some discourse communities have membership cards and newsletters), they are unaware of some, and they might deny being members of others.

A second preliminary issue is one we have touched on in an earlier chapter. Since it is a participant observer's goal to become, at least in some sense, a member of the group being studied, would it not be better if the researcher were a member of the group to begin with? This question has been asked repeatedly and answered in various ways. As Cassidy points out (1993), it was never resolved whether fieldworkers for the *Dictionary of American Regional English* should be insiders or outsiders to the communities in which they collected data. Some fieldwork in sociolinguistics has been especially effective because the fieldworkers were insiders [Clarence Robins's work with the Harlem teenagers studied by Labov (1972b) is one good example], and insiders sometimes believe—understandably, in some ways—that they are morally entitled to study "their" community in a way outsiders are not.

It may be that both insiders and outsiders can be effective. In any case, once they start working, participant observers are necessarily both insiders and outsiders (Spradley, 1980, pp. 53–62; Jorgensen, 1989, pp. 55–68), outsiders by virtue of occupying roles defined by themselves and other researchers and insiders by virtue of occupying roles defined by the people they are studying. A

researcher who remains completely outside the group, with no role
in it save that of researcher, is not doing participant observation;
on the other hand, being or becoming an insider to the extent that
it is no longer possible to maintain the critical and analytical distance necessary to abstract and generalize about the group is also
counterproductive. [Becoming too much of an insider is sometimes
referred to as "going native" or "becoming the phenomenon"; it is
discussed in more detail by Jorgensen (1989, pp. 62–65).] In many
groups, there are traditional roles for people who are in most ways
outsiders. In the United States, for example, school teachers and
university professors often come from outside the students' community. Ethnographer sociolinguists such as Shirley Brice Heath
(1983) are sometimes able to make use of this expectation, fitting
in somewhat the same way as a teacher would. Conversely, there
are often traditional ways in which insiders become outsiders. In
some communities, going to college or graduate school is an example. Being a graduate student meant, for example, that Julie
Lindquist (1995) was treated differently, in some ways, than other
bartenders in the local tavern where she studied working-class rhetoric, even though she was a community insider in other ways. In
the process of bantering with her about having acquired fancy ideas
in college, the bar patrons showed her important facets of their
understanding of how arguments work.

A related issue has to do with what sort of role the participant
observer adopts or is assigned in the community. As Jorgensen
(1989, pp. 53–55) points out, the "social location" of the researcher
affects what can be observed, how, and when. (The classic example is provided by the ethnography that purports to describe a traditional society but really describes only half of it, because the male
ethnographer had little or no interaction with women.) There is no
ideal social location; each possible role provides a different perspective. For this reason it can sometimes be useful to have different members of a research team take different roles. This appeared
to work well, for example, in my work with Judith Bean in Texas.
As a Texan with an obviously Texan way of talking and interact-
ing, Bean made the Texas women we interviewed feel as if they
would be understood and sympathized with; as a non-Texan with a
more reserved style, I encouraged them to be explicit about what
being Texans meant to them. Because I was assumed, like all Yan-
kees, to know very little about Texas (even after 10 years there), I

could ask dumb-sounding questions whose answers Texans might assume were obvious to other Texans. In our reading and observation, I noticed things that Bean, the insider, did not notice, and she was able to explain them in ways I could not. In a way that is more and more typical in ethnographies of the postmodern world, whether we are or are not "natives" is, in fact, not completely clear. Bean is a Texas woman by virtue of having been raised in Texas, whereas I am not; but I am a Texan, for some purposes, by identification. The more we come to see ourselves as "constructing" or choosing ways to be, the more the distinctions between "researcher" and "native," "emic" and "etic" begin to blur.

Starting Out: Field Methods
for Participant Observation

Ethnographers devote considerable attention to the beginning of the participant observation process, the crucial first steps of selecting an area and group to study, reviewing what others have written about it, and finding a way into the group. (A good guide is Agar, 1996b, Chapter 3.) The choice may be motivated mainly by area—you may have a part of the world in mind, or a specific group or research site that seems potentially interesting to begin with—or by theory (Agar, 1996b, pp. 73–75). If, for example, you start with a question about the relationship of urbanization and language change, your choice of a mobile, urbanizing population to study is dictated by your theoretical hunch. Obviously, your own background and predilections, as well as what your professional training leads you to think of as important, both influence the site-selection process, and it is wise to be as aware as possible of both sources of bias. The exotic feel that makes one research site seem fascinating may affect how you approach it and what kinds of things you expect to find, whereas the familiarity of another might keep some questions from getting asked because the answers seem obvious; questions framed with an eye to testing one theory about why people speak as they do may disguise other reasons for sociolinguistic variation.

Is it permissible to observe covertly, without people knowing what you are doing? Participant observers are divided on this issue. The casual, everyday observation that sometimes leads to research hypotheses is almost always covert, and the argument can be made that since people's behavior is not manipulated in participant observation research the way it is in interview or experimental work, participant observation does not really involve "human subjects" (Jorgensen, 1989, pp. 45–49). Furthermore, even when researchers make their purpose clear at the beginning of the project, people who have not been told are bound to wander onto the scene, and people who have been told may forget that they are being observed. Other researchers rule out covert participant observation, insisting that it is always unethical to pretend simply to be a participant when there is really a hidden agenda of observation—not to mention an agenda of analysis and relatively public description of the people in question. Clearly, the second stance is safer. Finding out after the fact that they have been "guinea pigs" can anger and offend people and potentially ruin any rapport with them. And people who know that they are being studied can sometimes contribute to the researchers' understanding of them in useful, unanticipated ways.

Sociolinguists are traditionally reluctant to trust what people say about how they talk, on the grounds that speakers' intuitions about the linguistic choices they make are skewed by their feelings about how they ought to speak. For this reason, participant observation aimed at describing language use has tended to rely less on interviews than ethnographies focused on other aspects of culture. If handled carefully, though, interviews can provide useful data.

Whether or not some research participants' explicit ideas about how and why they use language are elicited, it will almost always be necessary to choose a subgroup of people to study more intensively than others: people to tape, to work with in depth, and to use as case studies. Thus it is important to think carefully about whom to "use" in these ways. Newcomers to any community are likely to be approached first by what Agar (1996b, Chapter 6) calls "professional stranger handlers": people whose job it is, officially or unofficially, to approach outsiders or allow themselves to be approached. Think, for example, about moving to a job in a new city. It is likely that the first people you meet will be people who want to "sell" the new situation to you, in one way or another: your potential new boss or colleagues, followed by real estate agents or apartment locators or landlords. The way these people present and represent the community may be different from the way people you meet later will. In fact, once you have accepted the job and moved your household, people may actually say "Now we can tell you the truth!" Although there is no reason to rule out initial contacts as potential consultants and teachers, there is reason to think about their special roles.

In many settings, professional stranger handlers are people who are atypical in some way: the mayor of the town, the bilingual schoolteacher, people who want to work with you because they do not have a network of friends or relatives that keeps them busy, the best student in the class. As Labov (1972c) has most famously pointed out, there are "linguistic consequences of being a lame." People who are at the periphery of a social network are likely not to use language exactly the way core members are. [This point is also illustrated in the Milroys' (1987b) work on social networks in Belfast.] But there can be advantages to working with such people, as Friedrich (1986) shows: people who are unconventional may be able to play or create in ways that are revealing. Friedrich describes linguistic fieldwork in Mexico in which his informants included unusual, poetically virtuosic people. These informants enabled Friedrich to see, in relief, the ways in which speakers' choices are influenced by cultural and individual aesthetics (pp. 54–64).

What do the objects of participant observation get in return for your work with them? In research such as this, which crucially involves building rapport and being accepted as an equal, money may not be the best form of quid pro quo. Strategies for creating rapport in the first place include self-disclosure and joint activity with the people being studied (Jorgensen, 1989, pp. 75–78), and these may themselves be rewarding to research subjects, if they like having a new friend and collaborator. In the case of my and Judith Bean's work with Texas women, the possibility of publicity was a primary motivator and reward: since most of the women we were studying made their living as public figures, they appreciated having us talk about them (and some wanted us to use their real names).

Although this is not always clear from after-the-fact reports about it, ethnographic research almost always occurs in two phases, one relatively unplanned and exploratory, the second more systematic. (For graduate students, the first phase may result in a term paper, the second in a dissertation.) During the first phase, the researcher uses observations and, if appropriate, interviews to get a sense of what might be happening and what it might mean in local terms. To make sure, even in the early stages of research, that all aspects of the situation are noted, the development of heuristics—sets of things to make sure you notice, ask, or record, and strategies for doing so—is an important early step. "Scheduled" or semischeduled interviews, in which the interviewer refers to or has memorized a list of questions or topics, or systematic questioning strategies of other kinds, are useful in preliminary work with individual people. One kind of structured interview that has been used in ethnographic work (although it was created primarily for eliciting phonological information) is the sociolinguistic interview protocol designed by Labov (1984). For observing events in which language plays a key role, observational heuristics such as Hymes' SPEAKING paradigm are helpful. (This technique is discussed in the next section.)

As the researcher transcribes the first interviews or writes up the first observations, he or she begins to sense what the relevant analytical categories may be, based on what the research population says and does. To use examples from our work in Texas, we noticed early that people often talked about "sounding country," so we decided to find out more about what that meant and when and why it was done. When we asked young women how they would characterize Texans, they very often used the term "friendly," so we decided to explore what they meant by that and what the linguistic ramifications might be. We noticed that greetings were often very different from what one of us was used to, and that became the impetus for further study.

Once initial research questions are formulated in this way, the focus can be narrowed, using systematic techniques for refining the results of informal (but crucial) exploratory fieldwork. In the process, the researcher has to think about how to establish his or her authority to make claims and expect others to accept them. The idea of scholarly authority has been rightly critiqued for being based on the assumption that scholars (typically Western, or typically male, or typically from the "developed" parts of the world) automatically have the right to decide what is true about other people (typically non-Western, sometimes nonmale, often from the third world). Agar (1996b, pp. 13–15) argues that it is a mistake simply to give up on the idea of authoritativeness, because that would lead to cynicism and make scholarly inquiry pointless. Instead, says Agar, ethnographers should take explicit responsibility for the authoritativeness of their claims. This means, in part, talking about method, making the research process public so anyone could evaluate it

To make the research process public, it is crucial to be able to show that your results could be falsified (in other words, that you could have found a different result than you did). As Agar puts it, "Whatever you claim to be true, you set up some sort of test, a test where you can't control the outcome so that the results will confirm what you already suspect" (p. 43). Such a test may be quantitative ("Does x happen at least y percent of the time?"), but results can also be falsified in ethnography by listening to the details of how people talk about things, and sometimes by asking the people in question.

It is also crucial to be able to show how the patterns you find are distributed (in other words, when they occur, where, how often, and so on). Two things to consider in the process of making methods explicit are *sampling* and *distribution*. [See Agar (1996b, Chapter 7), for the extended discussion on which this paragraph and the next are based.] Sampling techniques are ways to make sure you are not just describing a few people and assuming without evidence that what is true for them is true for everyone in the group you are studying. In some cases, this can involve borrowing or inventing a quantitative way of testing hypotheses formed on the basis of a small sample. Although it is rare in sociolinguistics to use random samples, rigorously representative samples, including a predetermined number of people, events, or objects in each of a predefined set of categories, have been used. More often, samples are more loosely assembled. If the goal is (as it often is in sociolinguistics) in part to elicit relatively unselfconscious speech in fairly relaxed situations, using a network of friends or acquaintances in the way outlined by Lesley Milroy (1987a) has often proved useful. In his study of speech in Ayr, Scotland, for example, Macaulay (1991) used this technique, subsequently selecting for intensive analysis six interviews with middle-class people and six with working-class people. Jorgensen (1989) talks about "snowball sampling": starting with one situation and using your developing knowledge of it to identify other situations that are similar. This technique is useful when the relevant categories of analysis are not initially obvious. In any case, it is important to be able to describe and argue for the sample you choose or assemble. This means being able to talk about how you decided on the subset of people or events on which you focused and why that subset is likely to shed light on the larger set of people and events in the community you claim to be describing.

Thinking about distribution means thinking about averages and spreads. If you hear a certain feature or notice a certain speech event often, is it because everybody does it sometimes, or because some people do it all the time (and others not at all)? Or say that almost everyone does something a certain way: are the exceptions people who do it almost that way, or people who do it some completely different way? To find out, it might be useful to develop a standardized technique for noticing or eliciting the behavior in question: a standardized questionnaire or a test. As with sampling techniques, this need not (though it can) involve statistical tests, but must involve careful thought. Although it is important to question the idea that researchers are automatically entitled to claim that their interpretations are correct, a person who did not hope to learn more about the situation being studied than other people know would hardly have any reason to start. Researchers who can describe and defend their samples and detail the distribution of their claims create a basis on which others can evaluate their results, hence a basis for claiming authority.

Making Sense: Focusing Fieldwork and Analytical Methods

We turn now to the analytical methodology of ethnography: how to refine and interpret the observations and notes made, the texts and tape recordings collected, the pictures and films taken, and the information absorbed in the process of participant observation. Since the next chapter is more specifically about interpreting texts—records of talk, signing, or writing—we will concentrate here on the interpretation of "communicative events" that give rise to texts, keeping in mind that the two processes are in fact simultaneous and mutually informing.

One way of describing the goal of ethnography is that it should lead to "communicative competence," or the ability to function the way locals do in situations that involve talk and other forms of communication (Agar, 1996b, p. 131, note 12). Communicative competence is contrasted with "linguistic competence," or the ability to speak the local language(s) or varieties; that the latter does not imply the former is clear to anyone who has studied a foreign language for years but still is at a loss for what to say or how to act where the language is spoken. Ethnographers do sometimes acquire native-like communicative competence, blending in, sociolinguistically, in such a way as to be indistinguishable from insiders. But this is a goal that relatively few reach and not all wish to reach, and it is not always possible. More realistic may be the goal of being able to paraphrase what is going on, to "give an account" (Agar, 1996b, pp. 129–131), describing what is happening and why the way a local might. As Agar puts it, "to learn how informants give accounts is to learn the language. They become inseparable tasks" (p. 152).

The process of ethnography is often described as a funnel. As the researcher's hypotheses become more focused, observations become more focused, which in turn enables hypotheses to be focused further. In ethnography, data collection and data analysis are ideally concurrent and inform each other. In practice, particularly when it is not possible to be in the field for long or when the situation being studied does not last long, most of the formal analysis comes after the fieldwork; but informal analysis, in the form of thought and consequent revision of plans, is always part of the fieldwork phase. As Spradley (1980, p. 32) puts it in introducing his "Developmental Research Sequence," "both questions and answers must be discovered in the social situation being studied." Spradley suggests several criteria that are relevant in determining on what to focus as fieldwork and hypothesis formation progress. Focusing on aspects of the situation that spark your personal interest is obviously one, as is concentrating on aspects that are likely to be of theoretical interest. In my work with narratives in Indiana (Johnstone, 1990), my curiosity was particularly piqued by hearing people give extremely detailed specifications of locations that were more or less irrelevant to the plots of the stories they were telling, so I started asking myself more questions about that. Language and gender connections, on the other hand, did not originally strike me as particularly interesting, but partly because language and gender was a popular and productive topic at the time I eventually decided to explore that area as well. The people you work with may suggest things to consider further, saying things such as "If you really want to understand x, you should. . . . " For example, one of the Texas women to whom we were talking about sources of her style said, "I thought you were going to ask about mentors," which we then did. Practical considerations may have something to do with decisions about analytical focus. In Anne Johnstone's 1994 work in a university geology class, for example, the idea of exploring the instructor's responses to students' journal entries had to be revised when it turned out that the instructor was not reading the journals during the term. The focus-ing criterion that is hardest to define is "salience," the ways you begin to get a sense, as you observe, that some things are more important than others in local terms.

Good ethnography relies on lots of observation, systematic obser-vation, and observation of various sorts. As Agar (1996b, pp. 39–42) puts it, each pattern that is uncovered must be "massively over-determined" by data. However, you do not start with a checklist, including everything you need to consider and every angle to con-sider it from. So how do you ensure that you end up with enough, or good enough, evidence? Erikson (1986, p. 144) suggests some general strategies for making sure you do not miss too much, which I have adapted from his list:

- Alter the focus of your observations systematically from obser-vation to observation. In other words, take a different angle each time: watch a different person, go at a different time, sit in a different place, and so on.

- Make notes and take time to think after each observation. Do not let things pile up in such a way that you are not sure you remember what you saw or cannot remember what questions you wanted to ask. It is easy to imagine that your memories are going to be more indelible than they are. A good source of advice on taking notes systematically is Emerson (1995).

- Try various kinds of participation. Be a silent observer one time, talk to people the next. Present yourself as a university person one time, as a local the next (if you are in fact a local). Order a beer one time, a soft drink another time. And so on.

- Systematically look for discrepant cases. If "everyone" does something one way, try to search out someone who does it a different way.

- Include machine recording. In sociolinguistic work, audio-recording is almost always part of the research design. But it might be useful to videotape or audiotape interactions that are not meant to provide formal, transcribed data as well.

Erikson's heuristic for ensuring evidentiary adequacy is procedural, a set of things to do. Other useful heuristic devices are lists of things to observe. Spradley (1980, pp. 39–42), for example, suggests that in describing a social situation it is necessary at first to think systematically about *actors, activities,* and *place;* later, he adds *objects, acts, events* (that is, activities that are locally relevant), *sequencing, goal(s),* and *feelings* (p. 78).

A similar heuristic, geared specifically to the analysis of communicative events, is the list by Dell Hymes (1972) that has come to be known as the "SPEAKING paradigm" (though Hymes himself did not always present it as an acronymic list). Each of the letters of the word "speaking" corresponds to an aspect of a communicative event to which the analyst should pay attention, although in any given situation some will turn out to be more definitive than others.

- S stands for "setting." Some communicative events can take place almost anywhere, but for others the setting is crucial. For some Americans, for example, a wedding that takes place in a church is felt to be prototypical and proper, so that a wedding in a park or on a ski slope is taken to be an expression of resistance and/or creativity. University classes typically take place in classrooms, which are typically rooms with certain furniture oriented in certain ways. Classes that take place in other settings, such as outdoors, may be marked as more informal or meant for a special purpose. Resistance to the idea of having a class can be expressed by suggesting a move outdoors.

- P stands for "participants." A wedding must include two people who are to be married. Whether the two people must be a man and a woman is currently controversial; some Americans would not consider a two-man or two-woman event that was precisely like a wedding in other respects to be a "real" wedding. Classes traditionally require a teacher and several students.

- E stands for "ends," the purposes or goals of the participants and of the institutions that make the event possible or necessary. People may have multiple purposes, and purposes may be different for different participants. One reason for a wedding, for example, is to create a legal and/or ecclesiastical marriage. But weddings are also for socializing younger people, displaying wealth, and affirming, creating, or sometimes disrupting social bonds. From the perspective of the state, weddings regulate people by encouraging monogamy and child raising and serve to group people for the purposes of taxation, welfare, and so on. The purposes of a class are traditionally defined as teaching, for the teacher, and learning, for the students, so that teachers expect to do more teaching than learning and students more learning than teaching. This deep-seated ideology about the "ends" of a class creates room for challenge from alternative conceptions of pedagogy, but also makes alternatives hard to implement.

- A stands for "act sequence." This is a cover term for several things involved with what actually happens in what order. In a speech event, by definition, some form of discourse happens, sometimes at some particular time and sometimes throughout. The discourse itself consists of a sequence of utterances and words and a sequence of topics. The official part of a traditional wedding begins with the bride's procession up the aisle and often ends with a benediction from the officiating priest, pastor, or rabbi. The words that are spoken in the course of the wedding typically need to be spoken in a certain order, which is codified for some denominations in an "order of worship" particularly meant for weddings. Many classes start with the teacher's calling the group to order. This calling to order may start with "Okay, let's. . . . " During a class, people expect certain topics at certain times: summaries at the beginning, homework assignments at the end. Alternative orders are possible but marked.

- K stands for "key," or the overall register or tone of the event. A wedding may be formal or informal, but is it usually serious, not a joke. A response to an essay question in a class is typically not expected to be sarcastic in tone. Sometimes two communicative events can be differentiated only by their key. Failure to realize that a criticism is meant to be a joke or that a threat of suicide is serious can result in misunderstanding or much worse.

- I stands for "instrumentalities," or the media of communication typical of or required for the event. In Western culture, writing is often seen as the only way of creating lasting truth, so that something that is "in writing" can count in quite a different way than something spoken. Though weddings are mainly spoken (or signed), they usually involve at least one written document (a marriage license) and perhaps others (prayer books, poems), and they often—but less crucially—involve singing. In U.S. universities, written tests are more common than oral tests, which are typically reserved for ritual occasions in graduate school such as the dissertation defense. If actual instrumentalities are different from expected ones, an extra element of meaning is introduced. What, for example, might be the implications of a wedding over e-mail? Are classes ever sung?

- N stands for "norms" for interaction and norms for interpretation. Sometimes norms are overt, codified, and discussed; some are expressed as proverbs or mottos. The officiant at a wedding asks the questions, the people being married answer; this is rehearsed in advance, as are other aspects of people's expected behavior at weddings. Other norms are more covert. Women are, for example, expected in some traditions to cry at weddings, although this is not specifically stated or advised. In some traditions, getting drunk at the wedding reception and behaving in culturally expected drunken ways is a covert norm, officially discouraged but unofficially encouraged (via the availability of alcohol and the more general norm that people should "have a good time"). At a wedding, "I do" is traditionally interpreted as a promise, not a statement of a transitory feeling. "I hereby pronounce you husband and wife" is interpreted as a performative. Norms for interaction in a class result from prior expectations—that the teacher speaks first, that people do not get up and leave in the middle, and so on—together with explicit or inexplicit negotiation at the beginning of the semester and during its course. In some of my classes, for example, I make a rule on the first day that each student is to speak at least once each time; this rule is then either followed or flouted during the rest of the semester. In some classes, people speak simultaneously, in others not. Norms for interpretation in classes are the site of recurrent struggle, sometimes via overt questions, about assignments, for example ("What do you want us to do?") or about the relative importance of lecture and reading material ("Is this going to be on the test?").

- G, finally, stands for "genre," or the way(s) the event is categorized by the people involved. A wedding can be a kind of ceremony, a kind of church service, or a kind of mass; it is in the same category as other rite of passage events that result in lots of photographs, such as bar mitzvahs, graduations, or child-birth. Subordinate categories may be important, too: seminars, lectures, and recitations may be kinds of classes. Particular events often involve mixed genres: if people bring food to a class, it can become part party; a wedding can give rise to a family reunion and the expectations about setting, partici-pants, ends, act sequence, and so on that go with that genre.

Other potentially useful heuristics are suggested by Spradley (1980): ways of analyzing recurrent themes or relationships among key words and strategies for systematically generating questions to ask of your-self or others. Using this list, or any other, is no guarantee that you will think of and ask about everything. But such heuristics help in systematizing the process of observation and inquiry.

Ethnographic analytical techniques are often referred to as "unpacking" or "uncovering." They are more like the techniques of literary criticism, traditionally learned by reading and practicing and rarely discussed, than like the explicit procedures characteristic of quantitative research. As one book about the analysis of qualitative data puts it (Wolcott, 1994, quoted in Agar, 1996b, p. xi), "some of [the process] involves creative use of the imagination, mixed with empathy, rather than 'method' in any traditional sense of the term." The metaphors of unpacking and uncovering suggest that the mate-rial we analyze has layers, and that the more you peel away the closer to the center of things you are, the center of things being the native-like account of what is going on and the general ethical and epistemological principles that underlie it.

Another way of envisioning the process is to see the analysis as an attempt to start with incoherence and create coherence (Becker, 1995; Agar, 1996b, pp. 29–51). In the process of observation, moments arise that, to the researcher, seem to make no sense. (Agar calls these "rich points.") In everyday life, such moments are often dismissed as in fact incoherent (people say about a situation, "it was just crazy," and leave it at that), but ethnographers assume that for someone, on some level, there is always a coherent way of under-standing things. Agar suggests trying to find out what it is by try-ing out "frames," stories or nonnarrative structures of knowledge in which the events in question make sense, and then testing them and modifying them as necessary. A. Johnstone's (1994) *Uses for*

Journal-Keeping: An Ethnography of Writing in a University Science Class begins with a passage from a student's journal that might appear not to make sense: it is much shorter than the teacher's written assignment sheet specified, it is very casually spelled and punctuated, and it does not follow the assignment in several other ways. What, Johnstone asks, could have made the student make these choices? That question gives rise in the book, as it did in the research, to a variety of possible answers, some of which get rejected later and some of which are kept.

Thinking of culture as a set of ways of doing things rather than a set of facts people know, anthropologists increasingly think of ethnography as "narrative" rather than, as it was traditionally, "encyclopedic" (Agar, 1996b, pp. 8–13). What people say and otherwise do draws on shared knowledge, but it also subverts it, challenges it, and expresses individuals' ability to choose (Johnstone, 1996). Thus no ethnography can be comprehensive; the ethnographer must make choices about what to say and choices about how to write it—what plot or frame to use, what voice to adopt, how much room to give to the verbatim voices of research participants. So the question of "representation" in ethnography (van Maanen, 1995) is receiving more and more attention. Choosing what to write and how, it is argued, as much creates as reflects facts. Still, there are better and worse ways of writing ethnography, and the difference has a lot to do with the care and systematicity with which observations are recorded. Ethnographers often—traditionally, in fact—keep personal journals as well as field notes. This can help in providing a systematic way to encourage ethnographers to record both from a personal perspective, acknowledging the role of bias and emotion and fatigue in the process, and from a more "objective" perspective, attempting to use concrete language and be as detached as possible. In sociolinguistic work, it is often important to record (on tape or on paper) exactly what people say, not a paraphrase. It is important to make field notes about variation, too—to note who does not follow the pattern as well as who does, and what the differences are.

Summary

Ethnography is the description of how particular ways of being, acting, and talking make sense to the people who engage in them. The principal research technique of ethnography is participant observation: ethnographers' data are gathered in the process of becoming part of the groups they study, in certain ways, rather than by observing or manipulating their data from the outside. Explicitly or not, ethnographic research has always been a facet of sociolinguistic work, because sociolinguistics is rooted in the belief that linguistic variation is meaningful in communities of speakers, and that it is the fact that humans attribute significance to variation that drives language change. This chapter has outlined the interlocking processes of doing and analyzing ethnographic fieldwork, focusing in particular on the ethnography of communication. We have stressed the importance of starting out with analytical heuristics: systematic ways of ensuring that our observations are not biased toward our expectations or hopes.

DISCUSSION QUESTIONS

1. Find and read an article based on participant observation research. [You could use one of the chapters in Bauman and Sherzer (1989), all of which are ethnographies of communication, or find an article in *Language in Society*, the *Journal of Linguistic Anthropology*, the *American Ethnologist*, the *Journal of Sociolinguistics*, the *Journal of Pragmatics*, or some other sociolinguistics journal, in which case you will have to decide first which articles report on ethnographic work. Students could select the articles, or, to save time, the teacher could assign them.] Summarize the article for the class, focusing on its methodology. To what extent is methodology discussed? In what part of the article? Should there be more discussion of methodology? If so, what questions about the field and/or analytical methods would you like to have answered that were not? Evaluate the methodology, thinking about sampling and distribution and about evidentiary adequacy. Was a systematic attempt made to falsify the results?

2. Choose a recurring event in which speaking, writing, signing, or some combination is central (a "speech event," in Hymes' terms), and describe it in terms of the SPEAKING paradigm described in this chapter. Choose an event with which you are familiar

and to which you have easy access, but not one in which you have a central role. Observe the event at least once, making detailed field notes. Then, either orally or in writing, describe what typically and/or necessarily characterizes the event (what setting, participants, ends, act sequence, and so on) and in what ways the particular version you observed differed from this, speculating about why.

3. Have the teacher or a student perform some very short sequence of actions similar to but not identical to these: walk into the room and put down a book or walk around the table and open a window. Without discussion, everyone writes a sentence describing what just happened. Read the sentences aloud and compare them, focusing on the issues of bias and representation. What personal or cultural factors may have influenced how the incident was described? To what plots (culturally familiar stories) or frames (habitual ways of chunking ideas or events) was the incident adapted? Were any of the descriptions more "concrete" and/or more "objective" than others? Were there better and worse descriptions? (This idea is from A. L. Becker; it is described in Becker, 1988.)

SUGGESTIONS FOR FURTHER READING

General introductions to ethnography include Spradley (1979, 1980), Hammersley and Atkinson (1983), Erikson (1986), Jorgensen (1989), and Agar (1996b). A comprehensive survey of the various field methods ethnographers of communication can use is Saville-Troike (1989). Bauman and Sherzer (1974, later reprinted in 1989) remains an interesting and useful source of example studies in this framework.

◆ 8 ◆

Reading and Listening

DISCOURSE ANALYSIS

The term "discourse analysis" means different things to different
people, and courses and textbooks in this area vary widely. One reason is that discourse analysis is a relatively new branch of linguistics, with boundaries that have not been canonically fixed. Another
reason is that discourse analysis, unlike phonology or sociolinguistics, is not really a subdiscipline, but rather a methodology: it is an
approach to data collection and data analysis that can be used to
answer many kinds of questions, including those asked by sociolinguists. Discourse analysts do, of course, have research questions, but
they are often not particular to discourse analysis. Instead, they are
questions shared with people in linguistics and in other fields, questions about linguistic structure, about language change, about meaning, about language acquisition, about social roles and relations,
about communication, and about identity. What distinguishes discourse analysis from other branches of linguistics is not the questions discourse analysts ask but the ways they try to answer them:
by analyzing discourse—that is, by examining aspects of the form
and function of real samples of language use.

In this chapter we take a brief look at discourse analysis, thinking of it as a methodology with various uses for sociolinguists. To
do this we first need to decide what we mean by "discourse." Linguists do not completely agree, but a definition of "discourse" that
most would probably accept might be "language in use." Discourse
analysts study talk or writing or signing, language as it is "used" (or,

alternatively, comes to be) in actual interactions. More accurately, since it is nearly impossible to study linguistic interactions in real time as they are happening, discourse analysts study records of language in use: written texts or tapes and transcripts. Discourse analysis involves systematic reading and listening, in other words. In what follows, we think first about the field methods of discourse analysis—choosing and collecting written texts, tape recording, and transcribing—and then about analytical methods—how to read and/or listen systematically.

Recording Discourse

People who work with spoken or signed discourse almost always record it on audio- or videotape and then produce some sort of written version of what went on, called a transcript. Their analyses are then often based mainly on the transcripts. As we think about field methods in this area, then, we need to consider first the process of recording and then the process of transcribing. Both processes require more important decisions than may at first be obvious.

Sociolinguists sometimes feel that the only data that really count are tapes and transcripts, but using tape-recorded rather than purely observational data has advantages and disadvantages. As Erikson points out (1986), you cannot interact with a tape: unless you are part of the interaction being taped, you cannot, for example, stop people and ask them why they said what they just did, or get them to repeat something that is unclear. In addition, contextual information that might be important may be unavailable. Audiotape does not reveal whether people were looking at one another or how their bodies were aligned; even videotape shows only what the camera was aimed at. It is, of course, possible to alleviate these problems by being there when the tape is made and taking good notes—or having your fieldworkers take good notes—but even so there are bound to be questions that arise later. On the other hand, Erikson says, tape-recording can help make an analysis more complete and more fine-grained than a purely observational approach would. A tape you can hear or see over and over makes it possible to notice and take seriously things that happen only once, or rarely; in real-time observation we tend to notice things that are repeated. And a tape can help keep the analyst from jumping to conclusions that may be reinforced by selective memory. Baugh (1993) points out another advantage of tape-recording: the researcher does not have to be the one to collect the data, if he or she is not the ideal field-worker for the situation. For example, Baugh found in his own work with African-American street speech that his own English was too standard and made people speak in a more standard way to him than they might otherwise. So Baugh had other people do the tap-ing for him. This was also important in my work in Fort Wayne, Indiana (Johnstone, 1990), for which student fieldworkers taped their friends and relatives telling personal anecdotes in conversa-tion. As an English-department professor at the local university, I would have made people self-conscious and would perhaps have tended to elicit stories with explicit points about proper behavior. (My student fieldworkers were rewarded for their work in two ways: with course credit for the tape and a preliminary transcript of it, and with explicit acknowledgement in the book that resulted from the study.)

Often (though not inevitably or necessarily), sociolinguists see little point in studying discourse that occurred the way it did only because they set up an artificial situation and taped it. Even Dor-val (1990) and his colleagues, who studied videotapes of pairs of children who had been told to have a conversation while sitting side by side in an unfamiliar room across from a camera, had rea-son to believe that the children were still saying the same kinds of things in the same kinds of ways as they might in a less artificial situation. Sociolinguists are often interested, in other words, in studying relatively "naturalistic" discourse that is as close as possi-ble to what it would have been like if it was not being taped. Many well-known studies (such as, for example, Tannen, 1984) are based on tapes of "everyday" or "ordinary" conversation, the kind that goes on as people eat in groups or sit with friends.

If you imagine suddenly, in the middle of an intimate conversa-tion, setting up a tape recorder and ostentatiously reaching over to turn it on, or installing a video camera in the corner of the room and rearranging everyone so they are in the camera's range, you can see what the potential problems are: being on tape can make peo-ple embarrassed and self-conscious, make them start talking in unnatural ways or stop talking at all, make them cover their faces with their hands, or, alternatively, make them start showing off. With scenarios such as this in mind, researchers are often tempted by the idea of taping surreptitiously, via hidden equipment about which the researchees do not know. This technique has been used, and, as pointed out in Chapter 4, it may not always be illegal. But it is not a good idea. A very clear illustration why comes from Coates' (1996) study of "women talk." In 1983, before it was common in sociolinguistics to think systematically about "human subjects" ethics, Coates began surreptitiously taping a group of her friends. When Coates later told her friends what she had been doing, she was "staggered by their reaction: they were furious" (p. 5). Her friends were right to be angry, says Coates, as she had violated their rights as her friends and their trust.

If we cannot tape surreptitiously, is there any hope for naturalism in the data we collect? I think there is. The situation just sketched is a worst-case scenario; there are reasons to suppose that recording need not have such dire consequences for the quality of your data. For one thing, people living in the Western world now are very likely to be familiar with tape recorders and video cameras, and may well be used to being recorded. Not all 4 year olds have functional tape recorders with oversized controls, but some do, and others have seen ads for them; people whose parents do not videotape special moments at home may at least have been on camera at school. Many Americans seem to enjoy imagining themselves on TV, and wave as they pass a camera in a footrace or parade, or as a camera pans by in a stadium. People who are used to recording equipment may still be made self-conscious when a sociolinguist sets out to see how they talk, but not always. For example, Baugh (1993) claims that the people he tapes typically ignore the microphone, and many sociolinguists have had the same experience.

People's familiarity with recording equipment is one reason to suppose that its use may not completely change the way they act. Another reason is habituation: people get used to the machine after a while and sometimes even forget it is there. In the conversation excerpted below, three college-aged clerks at a shopping mall photo developing shop were talking to Tria Airheart-Martin, who was doing the taping, about good customers and bad customers. Steve, Ed, and Scott (all pseudonyms) moved back and forth between very natural-sounding conversational attempts to formulate and tell a story and stagy "for the tape" clowning with talk, as the tape recorder alternately got used as a resource in the conversation and then faded from the speakers' awareness. (Words in parentheses are ones Airheart-Martin and I were not sure of; empty parentheses replace material we could not make out at all. We return to the subject of transcription below.)

[Relatively unselfconscious talk: Ed tries to remind Steve of a story Steve could tell.]

STEVE: How about the uh "Are you trying to piss me off? Are you trying to make me angry?" person?

ED.   Oh but she wants a *good* story now. We're trying to think of (   )

TRIA: Oh that doesn't matter, just,

STEVE: (I don't have any) *good* story for her.

TRIA: just, any customer stories, either good or bad.

ED: Yeah. Tell, tell, yeah, tell,

STEVE: I don't have (too many that are) *good,* it's just (   ).

ED: Tell about the uh "Are you trying to piss me off?"

STEVE: That's right "Are you trying to make me angry?" (   ) tried to make me angry.

TRIA: Tried to make him angry.

STEVE: ((Imitating Dustin Hoffman in "Rain Man")) Uh-huh. Yeah.

   ((1-second pause))

[Awkward moment: Steve can't really remember the story or doesn't want to tell it, so the tape recorder becomes a resource for getting over the conversational hump.]

STEVE: What?

TRIA: Nothing. Huh!

ED: Gosh it's been so long you don't really remember it.

TRIA: Oh, oh, you're being sarcastic.

STEVE: ((directly into microphone, loudly)) *Hello!*

   ((Tria turns down recording volume))

   ((1–2 second pause))

   ((Tria laughs, turns volume back up))

[The tape recorder becomes the topic, around which a playful interlude about profanity gets constructed.]

STEVE: Is this on?

TRIA: Yes, it's on.

((Scott taps microphone))

TRIA: My instructor's going to be listening to this, I'll have you know.

ED: Oh really?

STEVE: And I've only been using, like, three words of profanity *per* minute.

TRIA: It doesn't matter. That's how you really talk.

STEVE: Damn damn damn.

TRIA: ((laughs)) Oh!

ED: There's no cussing in this store, (why are you saying) all that shit?

STEVE: Damn it!

TRIA: ((laughs))

SCOTT: So you want this goddamned bill done or what?

TRIA: ((laughs))

[Transition back to the story.]

SCOTT: Alright, serious.

TRIA: Okay.

[They start to formulate the story again, again sounding as if they were unaware of the tape recorder.]

SCOTT: Ahhh, let's see, what was happening? This person, what was she doing?

ED: I don't know.

SCOTT: Picking up, I believe.

TRIA: She didn't understand, uh, the copy negatives, process? She had you do copy negatives and you told her that it would lose quality? I think?

STEVE: No.

TRIA: No? Different person.

STEVE: (   ) on the phone wanted to know,

TRIA: Oh.

STEVE: why her reprints didn't match her original prints.

TRIA: Oh,

ED: (   ) copies

[The tape recorder is used as a resource in the performance of the story.]

STEVE: Aaand, well there are many reasons why, they do and don't, and I could fill up the entire, side of this tape—The entire side of this tape could be filled ((directly into microphone, mimicking a reporter)) with why it wouldn't work.

"What?" ((mimicking the customer))

But to make a long story short, after trying to explain it to her several times, and having her, I mean, we're talking, basic explanations like, "Different machines, different kind of prints. Simple as that, can't go into too much more detail than that because you wouldn't understand, different machines, different pictures."

"What? I don't understand." ((mimicking the customer))

"Different machines, different pictures. Okay, if you have two people drawin' a picture of, a horse then you're gonna have two different looking horses. Okay? That's the way it works. Different machine, different picture."

"What? I don't understand." ((mimicking the customer)) Fifteen times. Meanwhile I got customers backin' up behind this person, so finally I was lookin' at her "Are you just, trying to get me angry?" And she was givin' me this, "What?"

TRIA: ((laughs))

STEVE: "Well I'm, I'm just trying to figure out you know what, why you (   ) or if you're just trying to piss me off, 'cause, I know what I need to do so I can start helping these other people."

"I want your manager's name. Rr rr rr rr!" ((mimicking the customer)). . . .

There are people who are less casual about having their talk recorded than these young men and who would be less likely to make the experience into a playful resource for spontaneous conversation. But the bad customer transcript illustrates how easy it can be, contrary to what first-timers often expect, to get some people to talk into a microphone. What is probably more important than whether a tape recorder or camera is running is how the fieldworker manages the conversational ambience and encourages people, by example and through decisions about how to set up the scene, not to clam up or clown awkwardly. Tria Airheart-Martin, whose fieldwork for her customer-stories project was very effective, was perfectly open about what she was doing, even volunteering that her teacher was going to be listening to the tape. But she showed that it did not inhibit her, laughing and talking naturally, and that probably helped make Steve, Ed, and Scott less nervous about it.

Just as important as helping people feel comfortable about recording equipment is making sure the equipment works the way you want it to. For recording talk (unless you are interested in fine acoustic details), it is not necessary to use the most expensive tape recorder. Fairly small, book-sized models will work, as long as they record on full-sized cassettes.

If the people you want to record are fairly close to the tape recorder and likely to stay there, the machine's built-in microphone may be sufficient, though an omnidirectional microphone has the best chance of picking up all the voices around a table. Clip-on lavaliere microphones do the best job of recording the single speaker to whom they are attached, and, if you have the technical resources, it is possible to use multiple clip-on microphones, recording each speaker in a group on a different track. Keep in mind that background noise that people may not notice on the scene (the wind,

---

Box 8.1   A Hint About Tape Recorders

Minicassette tape recorders are meant for dictation—one person, speaking directly and at close range into the microphone—not for making high-fidelity recordings. They will generally not make usable recordings for sociolinguistics projects. Try to use a tape recorder that takes full-sized cassettes.

the TV, knives and forks hitting plates) is amazingly obvious and very distracting on tape, so try to see that the setting is quiet. And unless you can equip people with wireless clip-on microphones, try to get them to stay in one place.

The most important thing is to test your equipment on site before you start to use it. Record for 2 or 3 minutes, then stop the tape, rewind it, and play it back to make sure it is working and that you can hear everyone. Doing this may in fact help make people less nervous about being recorded, since they will know what the result sounds like. If it has the opposite effect, this will probably go away as people get involved in what they are doing and forget about the tape recorder. Similar considerations apply to people's comfort level with videotaping.

Kinds of Conversational Data

Airheart-Martin's data came from a conversation she initiated and in which she took part. It is thus in the middle of a continuum of ways researchers can be involved in their recordings. At one end of the continuum are situations in which the researcher is not present, having turned on the recorder and left or asked research participants to record themselves. If the researcher is an outsider to the community or situation, having people tape themselves may be the best way to proceed. Rampton (1995b), for example, had some of his school-aged consultants wear radio-microphones on the playground and in their youth club, to record interactions that might never have happened if an adult had been around, much less in the varieties of English and other langages in which they occurred. The danger, of course, is that the people we want to record have less invested in the process than we do, and may not make sure the tape recorder is actually recording, or turn the tape over when necessary, or even remember to turn the machine on in the first place. And a researcher who is not there has almost no effective control over what sorts of discourse go on, and how.

Also at the naturalistic end of the continuum are recordings of conversations that take place for some other purpose than sociolinguistic data collection. In our studies (discussed in Chapter 3) of gender and politeness and of apology, Ferrara, Bean, and I (Johnstone et al., 1992; Bean and Johnstone, 1994) worked with transcripts of public-opinion surveys that had been conducted over the phone. Kiesling (1997) recorded a fraternity business meeting, Ferrara (1994) worked with recordings of psychotherapists and their clients, Cushing (1994) analyzed radio conversations between airplane pilots and air traffic controllers, and Merritt (1977) studied transactions in shops. Radio, TV, and film have also provided sociolinguistic data. Apart from ensuring that the relevant permissions are obtained (particularly if the interactions are not routinely recorded), perhaps the most important fieldwork consideration is ensuring that the recording will be of high enough quality to be useful. Recordings of phone conversations, for example, depending on how they are made, may pick up only one speaker at a time, so would not be useful for studies of overlapping speech or interruption. Public places are often noisy, and noise that you unconsciously filter out in everyday life can turn out to mask what you are interested in, when taped. Again, make sure to try out the recording setup in advance.

At the other end of the continuum are recordings of more manipulated linguistic tasks. Airheart-Martin manipulated only the topic, saying, "Tell me about your worst customers." It is also possible to manipulate how speakers structure their talk, their styles, the varieties they use, even the words they say. Such manipulations are often accomplished in the course of interviews.

It is debatable to what extent an interview can approximate a "normal" speech event. In a study published in 1955, Strauss and Schatzman showed that many Americans did not know how formal, standardized survey interviews are meant to proceed, lower-class respondents being less likely than middle-class respondents to be familiar with the communicative expectations of this speech event. Wolfson (1976) shows how stories elicited in interviews are shaped around the necessity of answering the interviewer's question, and Briggs (1986) critiques the reliance of social scientists on interviews, illustrating the many ways people's expectations about normal talk are violated in interviews. Feminist social scientists have suggested that women may think of and behave in interviews differently than men (Finch, 1984; Oakley, 1981). But it can also be argued that the interview is an increasingly frequent and familiar speech event for most Americans, and perhaps for other people in the world as well. If your data consist of interviews, it is important to be able to justify their use in your particular context. Is there reason to suppose that the participants in your interviews are fairly comfortable with the situation? How can you tell this from their talk and other behavior? In the Texas Poll interviews we studied, for example, some people displayed their familiarity with the interview task by anticipating the interviewer's job, answering a multiple-choice question by saying "Number one," for example, rather than repeating the words they knew the interviewer would code by circling the numeral 1 on her form. This was good evidence, I thought, that at least for these respondents the task was a relatively "natural" one. What leads you to suppose that the varieties of talk your interview elicits are varieties speakers would use in other situations—or does it matter? What does it mean to say that some speech events are more "natural" than others?

Interviewing has a long history in sociolinguistics, of course, beginning with dialectologists' questionnaires (see Chapter 2). Oral questionnaires such as the ones used for the dialect atlases are relatively tightly structured interviews: each research subject gets asked the same questions, sometimes in the same order, and at least some of the answers have to have similar forms (a single word or a phrase). For this reason, as Baugh points out (1993), using a questionnaire can be a good way of making sure that everyone on a team of fieldworkers is doing more or less the same thing. Although questionnaires have usually been used to assemble large amounts of language-attitude information or large numbers of tokens of different ways of labeling things, the questionnaire interview is a conversation, and often includes stretches of monologue. So archived questionnaire tapes and transcripts may be a fruitful kind of data for discourse analysis. Pederson (1993) talks, for example, about how the tapes and transcripts resulting from the Linguistic Atlas of the Gulf States research could be used.

Quantitative studies of the correlates of linguistic variation, in the paradigm pioneered by William Labov, are based on data collected in interviews specially designed to elicit talk on a variety of topics and in a variety of styles, in the course of a relatively relaxed conversation. This kind of "sociolinguistic interview" is described in Labov (1984). The techniques involved would be better handled in detail in a book on quantitative sociolinguistics than here, since these interviews have most often been used to assemble statistics about how often people in certain predefined social categories (male or female, working class or middle class, central or peripheral to one's peer group) performing predetermined tasks (talking casually, reading aloud, reading lists of words) pronounce certain sounds. But transcripts of interviews designed in the Labovian way have been used as texts for discourse analysis (see, for example, Schiffrin, 1984, 1987; Macaulay, 1991), and other sociolinguists have borrowed from Labov's ideas. One frequently used part of the Labovian sociolinguistic interview has been the "danger of death question." On the theory that when people are emotionally involved in what they are saying they are likely to be less self-conscious and their speech thus more "vernacular," Labov and his colleagues ask people "Were you ever in a situation where you were in serious danger of getting killed?" Whether or not this question necessarily elicits a person's most unself-conscious speech (in some situations, it could turn out, a person narrating an often-told story such as this might have reason to perform it in a very artful way), it has proven to be a good way to get people to tell stories about personal experience.

But not all sociolinguists are interested in narrative, and interviews have to be designed to have the best chance of eliciting the kind or kinds of discourse in which the researcher is interested. It is easy to imagine that the "best" data for answering sociolinguistic questions come from the "best" interviews: ones that are relaxed, friendly, spontaneous sounding, like a good conversation. Sociolinguists *have*, in fact, devoted more attention to casual talk than to artful or formal modes, but this has had to do with the questions they were asking, not with the intrinsic worth of one kind of discourse over another. We can learn something about how language emerges and evolves from studying planned, careful talk, too.

Since it is often difficult to determine in advance exactly what a question will mean to the people you ask, it is a good idea to try out, or "pilot," your interview with one or two subjects before starting the full-scale project. This way you can find out in time if a question you thought would really get people talking elicits only a "Yes" or an "I don't know," whether people speak as formally or as casually as you expected them to, and so on. Pilot-testing an interview format also helps you see what kind of an interviewer you are, whether, for example, you are prone to letting the conversation wander and take longer than you told the interviewee it would, or whether you are the sort of person who insists so vehemently on sticking to the plan that you risk missing interesting other topics or styles. It may be wise to remember that you can get comparable data from different people without having exactly the same conversation with each one. On the other hand, it is important to keep in mind what you are trying to accomplish with the interview.

There are of course other ways of eliciting spoken or signed language, either to supplement interviews or instead of them. For example, people can be asked to perform some task and talk about it. Chafe and his colleagues (1980) had people watch a short film and then asked them to tell what they had seen. Sociolinguists have also asked people to listen to tapes or look at pictures.

Transcribing

Here is the first section of the "bad customer" excerpt from above again:

> STEVE: How about the uh "Are you trying to piss me off? Are you trying to make me angry?" person?
>
> ED: Oh but she wants a *good* story now. We're trying to think of ( )
>
> TRIA: Oh that doesn't matter, just,
>
> STEVE: (I don't have any) *good* story for her.
>
> TRIA: just, any customer stories, either good or bad.
>
> ED: Yeah. Tell, tell, yeah, tell,
>
> STEVE: I don't have (too many that are) *good*, it's just ( ).
>
> ED: Tell about the uh "Are you trying to piss me off?"
>
> STEVE: That's right "Are you trying to make me angry?" ( ) tried to make me angry.
>
> TRIA: Tried to make him angry.
>
> STEVE: ((Imitating Dustin Hoffman in "Rain Man")) Uh-huh. Yeah.

Apart from the material in parentheses (the words and phrases we were not sure we understood), this transcript looks like a play script. This way of transcribing the excerpt makes it look as if one person had spoken at a time, waiting to start until the last person was finished and there was a pause. In fact, this was not what happened (and it is rarely what happens in any conversation), as an alternative transcript of the same segment shows:

> STEVE: How about the uh "Are you trying to piss me off? Are you trying to make me angry?" person   =
>
> ED: =   Oh but she wants a
> *good* story now. We're trying to think of   [(   )
>
> TRIA: [Oh that doesn't
>   [matter, just,
>
> STEVE: [(I don't have any) *good*
> story for her.
>
> TRIA: just, any customer stories, either good   [or bad.]
>
> STEVE: [I don't have]
>   [(too many that are) *good*, it's just (   ).]
>
> ED: [Yeah. Tell, tell, yeah, tell]   Tell about the
> uh "Are you trying to piss me off?".
>
> STEVE: That's right "Are you trying to make me angry?" (   )
> tried to make me angry.
>
> TRIA: Tried to make him angry.
>
> STEVE: ((Imitating Dustin Hoffman in "Rain Man")) Uh-huh.
> Yeah.

In this transcript, equals signs show when a second speaker "latches" onto a first, starting to talk immediately with no pause. Lined-up brackets (sometimes typeset as long brackets actually connecting two lines) signal the beginning of simultaneous talk and sometimes the end. In addition to making it clear why some of the talk on the tape was hard to hear (it was almost always being said at the same time someone else was talking), this transcript shows exactly when speakers' turns started, who talked at the same time, and when they stopped. In these ways, this version is more realistic than the first one. But it is also much harder to read, and the additional information about latching and overlap that decreased its readability was not relevant to my discussion, earlier, about how the tape recorder got used as a resource in this conversation. So I decided to use the play-script version instead.

Transcription always involves choices such as this. A transcript is necessarily a partial representation of talk, and transcribers have to decide what information to include and what to leave out. These decisions have practical and theoretical consequences. As Ochs (1979) points out, transcription choices are theoretical. (See also Edwards and Lampert, 1993; Tedlock, 1983.) For example, a transcription system that highlights interruption and simultaneous talk (such as my second version) makes it relatively easy to think of conversation as collaborative, whereas a play-script transcript makes it look more as if each speaker had an independent conversational agenda. And, as we will see, choices about how to punctuate people's speech and spell their words are choices about how to represent social status, linguistic ability, and character. Practically speak-

---

Box 8.2 Transcription Hints

No matter what format you choose for transcribing, a few simple steps will make the transcription easier to read and refer to.

- Use actual, spelled out names for the speakers, not initials. (These should generally not be their real names, of course, but rather pseudonyms.) It is much more difficult for the reader of a transcript to keep track of who is talking when the speakers are labelled "A," "B," and "C" than when they are "Anne," "Bruce" and "Callie." If you decide to let research participants choose their own pseudonyms, remember that readers may find names easier to keep track of than labels that are not names: "Callie" will probably be less distracting, for example, than "China Girl" or "spiderwoman."

- Number the lines of the transcript so you can refer the reader to the precise parts you discuss in your presentation or paper. "Line 36" is much easier to find than "the third line from the top on the second page" or "the part where Anne says 'In my opinion.'"

- In excerpts from transcripts that you use as examples, highlight the relevant lines, words, or phrases so readers can pinpoint exactly what to focus on. Use arrows in the margin, or, on a handout, perhaps a typeface that you are not using for any other purpose.

ing, highly detailed transcripts are often hard to read, whereas easy-to-read transcripts include less specific information. Interdisciplinary discussion about the best way to transcribe can become heated, as Luebs (1996) has shown, even though no technique could possibly be "correct" for all purposes.

Let us look at some of the choices a transcriber has to make in deciding how to represent a single speaker's speech. One set of choices involves punctuation marks. People do not speak in sentences. The sentence is a unit of orthography, not a unit of speech, so even when speakers produce complete grammatical units (as they often do), deciding which groups of these constitute "sentences" is necessarily somewhat arbitrary. As Chafe (1980) has shown, people appear to speak in chunks of around seven words at a time. Most of these chunks end with falling or rising intonation, and, in monologue, a pause, and most of the chunks are complete phrases or clauses. But the need for processing time as a speaker plans the next chunk, as well as things such as stress or interruption, can interfere with the flow of discourse, with the result that talk is full of hesitation, repetition, incomplete phrases and clauses, backtracking, and words like *um* and *uh*. Most transcribers use conventional punctuation marks—commas, periods, question marks, and so on—to represent aspects of how talk flows and stumbles along. It seems intuitively to make sense to use a comma to signal a pause, a period to signal a more final-sounding pause accompanied by falling intonation, and a question mark for phrase-final rising intonation.

Traditionally, however, punctuation marks signal facts about syntax as often as (or more often than) they signal facts about what speech sounds like. For example, periods are meant to go at the ends of grammatically declarative sentences, even if the sentence may sound like a question. Thus, when transcribing what McLemore (1991) calls "uptalk," the use of rising intonation at the ends of declarative utterances, transcribers have to choose between the standard, grammatical option, using periods, and the acoustically more accurate one, using question marks. Compare these two transcripts to see what the effects of such choice can be:

(8.1a) I was in Albertson's?
        and I saw this guy I knew from class?
        an' he goes you wanna have dinner?
        an' I'm like SURE.

(8.1b) I was in Albertson's, and I saw this guy I knew from class, and he goes, "You want to have dinner?" And I'm like, "Sure."

Transcript (8.1a) shows the speaker's uptalk pattern, and divides the discourse into lines, as if it were poetry, to represent the chunks in which it was uttered. Since there was nothing about the intonation that corresponded to the beginnings of the speaker's representations of the young man's speech or her own, quotation marks and the accompanying standard quote-introducing commas are not used. The capital letters show that the speaker said "sure" in a louder voice. Transcript (8.1b) is in standard written format, as it would appear, for example, in a novel. "An'" and "wanna" are "corrected" to "and" and "want to," and punctuation is used the way writers' handbooks say to use it.

Clearly, transcript (8.1a) is more accurate than transcript (8.1b) when it comes to showing what the *talk* sounded like. But note how the *speaker* comes across. In (8.1a) she seems sloppier, less grammatical, and more excitable than in (8.1b). The use of nonstandard orthography suggests that the speech, and, by implication, the speaker are nonstandard, when in fact the excerpt is in completely standard spoken English.

As Dennis Preston has pointed out (1985), some of the intentional misspellings that seem to suggest nonstandard speech are in fact partly phonetic spellings of perfectly standard ways of pronouncing things. "An'," for example, in transcript (8.1a) above, represents the way people regularly say "and" when the next word begins with a consonant. "Wanna" is an example of what Preston calls an "allegro form," a spelling that represents the kinds of elision and deletion that occur in connected speech in all varieties. If I had decided to spell "sure" in the example as "shur," this would have been "eye-dialect," a partly phonetic respelling of the way the word is always pronounced. Nonstandard spellings sometimes really are attempts to represent nonstandard pronunciations, so that, for example, a Southern American might be transcribed saying "neked" for "naked" or "purty" for "pretty."

To see the effect of different choices about spelling nonstandard pronunciation, let us look at three versions of a short passage from Zora Neale Hurston's *Their Eyes Were Watching God* (1937). Excerpt

(8.2a) is Hurston's version; (8.2b) and (8.2c) are rewrites of the same passage.

(8.2a)   Ah don't even b'lieve Jody b'lieve dat lie. He ain't never took no stock in de mess. He just make out he b'lieve it tuh hurt me. Ah'm stone dead from standin' still and tryin' tuh smile.

(8.2b)   I don't even believe Jody believe that lie. He ain't never took no stock in the mess. He just make out he believe it to hurt me. I'm stone dead from standing still and trying to smile.

(8.2c)   I don't even believe Jody believes that lie. He hasn't ever taken any stock in the mess. He just makes out he believes it to hurt me. I'm stone dead from standing still and trying to smile.

Though "local color" fiction that represented regional speech through elaborate respelling was popular and uncontroversial in the nineteenth century, by the time Hurston wrote in the 1930s it was less common, and many contemporary writers find it objectionable. Sociolinguists are, of course, often interested in the particulars of how words sound, and a text such as Hurston's might be useful for the suggestions it makes about how African-Americans in Florida may have sounded before the days of widespread taping. If a sociolinguist were doing the transcribing, though, he or she would be likely to use the International Phonetic Alphabet (IPA) for phonetic detail that was especially worth noting. It would also be relatively unlikely, however, for a sociolinguist to make the kinds of grammatical changes that have resulted in version (8.2c), in which nonstandard syntax has been replaced by standard forms. Some of our own habits of thought about the normal way to transcribe may be more conventional and less reasoned than we suppose.

To summarize, here are some of the things transcribers should ask themselves before deciding how to proceed:

1. What sorts of theoretical bias are suggested by the system you have in mind? (For example, transcribing in lines suggests

that talk is like poetry; showing lots of overlapping talk suggests that talk is collaborative work, and so on.)

2. How do the choices you have in mind represent the speakers whose voices you are transcribing? (Do you write "wanna" or "want to"? "Writing" or "writin'"? When do you use the IPA? Here you have to strike a balance between accuracy or realism and the kinds of characterization that are implied in every possible choice.)

3. What is the transcript for? What are you going to look at in it? What do you need to be able to highlight when you present it to others? What does your audience need to be able to see? Remember that a tape or an extract can be transcribed different ways for different purposes.

Using Written Texts

Much of the work of sociolinguists is about spoken language. But people's writing can also show how their language and their social world shape each other. It can be argued, in fact, that a complete view of the sociolinguistic competence of an individual or a social group, if the individual or the group lives in a literate world, must include a study of how they write and how they use writing. The point of Heath's (1983) work in two Southern communities, for example, was to examine how forms of literacy emerged out of and created forms of talk, and how home literacy intersected, or did not, with how reading and writing were used in schools. As part of her ethnographic work in "Trackton" and "Roadville," Heath collected and studied things people wrote—shopping lists and cards—and things they read—magazines and letters.

Many other studies have been based on such "found" written data: written texts that were already there, that would have existed whether or not the sociolinguist had decided to study them. For example, Becker's (1975) analysis of how the Burmese grammatical classifier system creates "a linguistic image of nature" was based partly on a book of lists that Becker's Burmese–language teacher gave him. In an article based on her doctoral dissertation, Schnebly (1994) studied how repetition in conversation can suggest anomie and desperation, using as her data play scripts by "theater of the absurd" playwrights Pinter and Albee. Some sociolinguistic studies are based on large written corpora, consisting of hundreds of texts. One example is Biber and Finegan's (1989; Biber 1988) work on the evolution of written style in English; others are described in Stubbs (1996).

Other studies have been based on elicited written data: texts that were written because sociolinguists asked people to write them. Tannen (1982), for example, compared syntactic choices in written and spoken media by having people tell a story and then, several weeks later, write the same story, or, alternatively, to write the story first and then tell it later. For a dissertation exploring connections among gender and ethnicity and narrative style, McLeod-Porter (1991) asked middle school students to write about themselves.

There are as many ways of finding and selecting written texts as there are ways of studying them, so there are few (if any) specific rules about field methodology for this kind of work. In discourse analysis as in ethnography (Chapter 7), it is important to think about whether and how the texts you select represent the range of texts you claim to be studying, and it is important to avoid making overly large claims on the basis of not enough data. Particularly for discourse analysts who rely on the close-reading analytical methods to be described below, it is often impossible to deal with large quantities of textual data. So claims about what you find have to be phrased as suggestions, and you have to think carefully about which aspects of what you find might be generalizable to other texts. One thing that may have to be considered in advance was mentioned in Chapter 4: published writing is often copyrighted. In general, people are allowed to study and write about others' published writing without obtaining their permission to do so (literary criticism would be problematic if this were not so), although if you want to study unpublished material, or talk to writers about their writing, or use their discourse in other media as well, you need to have their informed consent. But it is often necessary to get permission from copyright holders to quote more than a sentence or two from published work, and it is hard to present the results of a study of a written text without quoting from the text. Copyright law is fluid and in some cases unclear, particularly when it comes to electronic texts, and publishers and authors have been known to charge steep prices for permission to quote, even when the quotes are for scholarly purposes and do not apparently threaten to undermine the value of the original publication. And some authors and publications will not permit any quotation, for any purpose. So it is wise to look into this issue before starting out.

Analytical Approaches

There are, of course, many ways to analyze discourse. One set of ways is quantitative, involving counting up features that occur in texts or transcripts (simultaneous speech, uses of the historical present, repeated phrases, or whatever), tabulating the results, and com-paring them with results for other texts or other parts of the text. This kind of work, although it is not the subject of this book, is often part of studies that are in the main qualitative. Finding out how often something happens can be a way of generating questions that can be answered by means of the reading and listening tech-niques on which this book focuses. For example, one influential early study about language and gender was Zimmerman and West's (1975) quantitative analysis of instances of simultaneous speech in conversation, on the basis of which they claimed that in mixed-sex conversations, women are interrupted more often than men. This study was part of what gave rise to Tannen's (1994, pp. 53–83) qual-itative, ethographically sensitive study. Tannen showed that the issue is actually more complex than Zimmerman and West thought, since not all simultaneous speech actually counts as interruption to the speakers involved. Tannen's conclusions could not have been reached by counting, but they were in some ways sparked by it.

Each approach to the analysis of discourse involves analytical heuristics of one sort or another. My own early training in discourse analysis (though I did not call it that then) was in lessons about interpreting literature in secondary school English classes, where the heuristic I remember learning first was "Look for the metaphors and similes." That heuristic was one of the analytical tools of the New Critics, whose focus was on the details of the internal struc-ture of texts. Subsequent schools of literary criticism have proposed other heuristics, such as "Look at what the reader has to do in mak-ing his or her own sense of the text," "Look at what the text meant when it was written," "Concentrate on what is presupposed by the words of the text or not said at all," "Concentrate on the female characters," "Concentrate on how the text represents or fails to rep-resent dominance and oppression," "Pay attention to the ways in which the text 'deconstructs' itself through ambiguity," and "Study the author's biography."

If any one of these heuristics is used to the exclusion of others, the result can be a one-dimensional and hence and rather thin interpretation. What we need is a way to make sure we are systematically paying attention to a variety of reasons why a stretch of discourse might have turned out the way it did. One way of doing this has been suggested by A. L. Becker (1995). Becker's technique involves thinking systematically, one by one, about a variety of "sources of constraint" on discourse: reasons, that is, why texts have the forms and the functions they do, and not other forms and functions. (Note again that we are not just talking about written "texts" here, but about discourse in any medium. A text could be a single sentence or a conversation or a poetry reading.) Becker's system is a flexible one; he describes it somewhat differently in different places. What follows is one adaptation of it.

Discourse Is Constrained by the World. This is the source of constraint most people think of first. Discourse is shaped by what it is about and how it is related to interlocutors' "worldview," or to the world speakers and writers think of as independent of language. What kind of world is created in the text? One in which people are actors or acted upon? [See Hodge and Kress (1993) on how transitivity, the passive, and the use of equational sentences can create different patterns of agency in texts.] One in which people are metaphors for machines or one in which machines are metaphors for people? One in which mountains are things or one in which mountains are events?

Discourse Is Constrained by Language. Speakers tend to do what languages make it easy to do. And the nature of language itself, the fact that on every level wholes are built from smaller parts, makes it possible for people to begin with sounds and end up with wars or marriage proposals or TV talk shows. To produce or interpret discourse, a person has to know how to produce and interpret sentences in a language (or more than one language, or a mixture of languages). He or she also has to have made some generalizations about discourse-level rules for structure: narratives often start with summaries of what is to come, conversations are often organized around the principle of turn-taking, thematic ("old" or "given") information tends to come at the beginnings of sentences, *because* can be used to make texts cohesive on a variety of levels, and so on. Thinking about this source of constraint (or of creativity, of course: people can break the rules) reminds us of how grammatical "rules" are often (perhaps always) the result of discourse strategies: strategies for trying to make sure others can interpret what you say and for interpreting what others say.

Discourse Is Constrained by Speakers/Writers/Signers, Addressees, Audiences. What someone says and how is influenced, that is, by who the audience is, who the speaker is, what the relationships between speaker and hearer are, who else is listening, and how speaker and audience are related to them. Asking questions about discourse participants helps make us aware of the effects on discourse of social roles and relations, of how power, gender, ethnicity, and more specific, particular identifications are constructed, contested, and displayed as people talk and interpret talk. It helps make us aware of the ways discourses are designed for, and in some cases partly by, their audiences, and of how people accommodate one another's styles and expectations, or fail to. It also raises questions about the role of "society" vis-à-vis individual speakers and interpreters: to what extent are what we say and how we understand determined by forces outside us that speak through us, and to what extent are individuals responsible agents?

Discourse Is Constrained by Prior Discourse. What people expect to hear in a given context, how they expect it to be said, and what they expect it to mean are also important shapers of discourse. Speakers evoke things previous speakers have said and expectations about how to interpret their utterances. Asking about prior text means asking about how the setting of discourse (in a newspaper, on the floor rather than in a chair, on stage) is connected to what discourse is taken to mean. It means asking about "genre," seen both as expected form (the rhyme scheme of a sonnet or the question–answer structure of an interview) and as expected ways of adapting to purpose (authors of academic journal articles use abstracts to introduce their major claims; conflict mediators start by trying to define the problem at hand). Asking about prior text means asking about "discourses" in the plural: the ways of thinking and talking that circulate in our social environment, and on which we unthinkingly or purposely draw. It means asking about how much of a text is formulaic and how much is new, how much is repeated and how much is not.

Discourse Is Shaped by Its Media of Production and Reception. A text is shaped in part by whether it is spoken or written or signed, transmitted electronically, and so on. Writing is different in structure, in purpose, and in effect than speaking, and signing is different from either; electronic communication is like speech in some ways, like writing in others, and like neither in many ways. And one medium cannot be made to duplicate another: an e-mail correspondence can approximate a spoken conversation but never be completely the same. Writing on stone is different (slower, for one thing) than writing at a keyboard; printing makes possible different kinds of writing than were possible when manuscripts were copied by hand; groups of deaf children who sign can be silently rowdy, whereas hearing children for whom rowdiness involves yelling almost always call adults' attention to their misbehavior.

Discourse Is Shaped by People's Purposes.   What speakers, hearers, and audiences are trying to accomplish also influences what their discourse is like. Thinking about purpose, and about interpretations of purpose, means thinking about speech acts intended and understood, about the strategic, rhetorical aspects of texts and text-builders, about "registers," or ways of speaking and writing that key speakers' intentions. It means thinking about meaning from multiple perspectives: meaning by speakers, meaning to audiences, and indeterminate meaning that shifts depending on one's goals as a hearer or reader.

Summary

Discourse analysis is the close, systematic analysis of written texts or records of speech or signing. Collecting the data for discourse analysis often involves audio or videorecording, together with transcription. Situations to record range from the completely naturalistic to the relatively manipulated. Interviews, which are along the manipulated end of the continuum, have been a common source of sociolinguistic data, but many other kinds of spoken, signed, and written data have been used, too. Analyzing texts or transcripts requires paying systematic attention to all the reasons they take the shapes and have the functions they do. With the possible exception of "explication de texte" exercises in literary analysis, however, discourse analysts do not simply choose texts and then analyze them. Instead, analyses of discourse are always focused on research questions. So not every source of constraint will turn out to be equally relevant for every project. You may, for example, be specifically interested in the connection between language and gender, and thus focused on the roles of speakers and hearers in discourse, or you may be interested in genre and thus focused on prior text, or you may be particularly interested in how purpose and discourse are related, because you are concerned with the rhetorical dimensions of discourse. But although your analysis will probably not be an exhaustive account of all the possible reasons your text is the way it is, it is vital to keep in mind that the kinds of reasons you are examining are not the only ones in play.

DISCUSSION QUESTIONS

1. Tape-record at least half an hour of a conversation among friends or family, getting people's informed consent first. Transcribe 5 minutes of the tape (not the first 5 minutes: wait until the speakers have relaxed a bit). Here are some things you will need to think about as you do this and which could be discussed in class:

   a. What was the participants' reaction to the fact that the conversation was being taped? Did the tape recorder make people self-conscious at first? If so, did it continue to have this effect throughout the conversation?

   b. What technical problems, if any, did you have, and what did you decide to do about them? Could the recording quality have been better? Did people move out of range of the microphone? What would you do differently next time?

   c. What decisions were involved in deciding how to transcribe the segment? What is lost and what is gained by the system you chose? Did transcription take the amount of time you expected it would?

d. What did you learn from doing this exercise?

2. Design an interview meant to (a) elicit a range of a speaker's styles, from fairly formal to fairly casual, and (b) elicit the speaker's sense of how his or her region of origin affects the way he or she talks, if it does. This interview will be partly sociolinguistic (meant to elicit variation in speech) and partly ethnographic (meant to elicit information about culture). Your interview should be at least loosely based on a set of questions and/or tasks that you would have each subject answer or carry out. Try out your interview on one speaker and evaluate it. What would you do differently the next time?

3. It is often claimed that electronic conversation—e-mail and on-line chatting—is in between writing and talk in some ways. Here is an excerpt from the printout of an electronic chat.

Stodoe: Are you at work?

nye3407: No in my room

nye3407: I'm just messaging someone on the vax at teh same time

nye3407: what have you been up to lately

nye3407: besides lot's of work

Stodoe: Oh I'm doing the same. It's too complicated.

nye3407: Yeah, but it's fun

Stodoe: My mom visited this week. Saturday was good because I had time to see her but then on Sunday I was trying to do work and she kept talking to me and I felt like, hmm, how shall we say, AAAARRRGH.

Stodoe: That's true.

nye3407: The reason my parents don't visit

Here are a few of the questions we might ask about this data:

a. Should this printout be treated as a written text or as a transcript? What would be the ramifications of treating it either way? For example, would it ever be desirable, when writing about this extract, to use real names instead of "nye3407" and "Stodoe" or to correct the spelling and punctuation so the "speakers" would look less non-standard?

b. What can you tell about the relationship between the two interlocutors from this excerpt? How can you tell?

c. What questions does the excerpt raise about the effects of the medium on discourse? In what ways is this like a conversation, in what ways is it like an exchange of written notes, and in what ways is it like neither? Think about the topic, the sentence structure, conventions for turn-taking, and how paralinguistic information such as volume is represented. What can people do in this medium that they cannot do in others, and what can they not do?

4. Select a short written text—a paragraph or less—and use the Becker heuristic to raise and try to answer questions about why the text is the way it is. Ask yourself "Why does this text consist of these particular words, represented on the page in these particular symbols, in this particular order?" and try to generate as many answers to this question as you can.

SUGGESTIONS FOR FURTHER READING

Introductions to discourse analysis include Brown and Yule (1983), Renkema (1993), Stubbs (1983), Schiffrin (1994), and van Dijk (1997), although each delimits the field differently and only Schiffrin treats discourse analysis primarily as a methodology, as I do here. An interesting collection of articles about transcription is Edwards and Lampert (1993). Many chapters in Becker (1995) are organized as systematic applications of the analytical heuristic I describe in this chapter to small bits of discourse, showing how it is possible to work outward from a phrase or a sentence to an understanding of language and culture in general.

◆ 9 ◆

Writing

One of the products of sociolinguistic research is almost always at least one written document: a term paper, notes or a "talkscript" for a conference presentation, a dissertation, a journal article, a book chapter, or a book. Many reports of qualitative sociolinguistic projects have the more or less traditional format of a social science article. But traditional article format is not the only option for reporting the kind of work we do, and there are habits of wording and phrasing associated with reports of large-scale quantitative work that are not really appropriate for talking about work done in a more particularistic, detailed, humanistic paradigm. In this chapter we consider some of the options for writing about qualitative sociolinguistic research.

The Article

The structure of academic research reports has itself been the subject of sociolinguistic research connecting genre, discourse community, and discourse structure. A key example is Swales (1990). Although most of this research has used reports about quantitative research as data, often in the sciences or engineering, an author's rhetorical tasks in writing an article are very much the same across disciplines. Although its specific format can vary, sometimes depending on the requirements of a teacher or a journal, a research report in the social-scientific mode typically includes the following sections. Sections are often labeled and graphically separated by blank lines.

Abstract. Before the article proper begins, many journals require a short (150–250 word) summary called an abstract. This helps readers decide whether the article is relevant to their interests and whether it needs to be read in its entirety. The abstract is usually fairly impersonal in tone. It talks about what *the paper* does rather than about what *the author* did. (The abstracts of three of the four articles in the March 1998 issue of *Language and Society* begin the same way: "This article considers," "This article proposes," and "This article examines.") Because of the need for brevity, the abstract is often more complex in syntax than the actual article. The abstract should mention all the sections of the paper and it should outline the significance of the findings. Although abstracts for conference papers (on the basis of which proposed presentations are accepted or rejected) are, by necessity, often written before the paper they supposedly summarize, article abstracts are written afterward, often drawing the ideas for one sentence or two from each of the article's main sections.

Introduction. The introduction is a crucial part of the paper, and often the hardest part to write. Its rhetorical function is to draw readers into the topic, to make them see why it is important and what you have to say about it that is new and interesting. Swales (1990, pp. 140–166) describes the process as having three rhetorical steps. The first is to establish the general territory in which you are working. This can be done in several ways. One traditional way to begin is by emphasizing the importance of the general topic by briefly reviewing previous research in the area and making generalizations about what has been found. The second step is to establish a specific niche for yourself in that general area. This can be done by making a counterclaim to a previous researcher's claim. Because of the interpretive nature of qualitative work, it is rare— and accordingly, perhaps risky—to claim that someone else is simply wrong. More usually, a counterclaim is described as a different way of explaining things, not as the right way as opposed to the wrong one. You can also establish a niche by indicating that there is a gap in previous research. If you choose this option, remember that the people whose work you are talking about may be reading yours, so rather than talking about what other people have "failed" or "neglected" to do, it is wise (and polite) to describe the gap your work fills in a way that is as respectful as possible of the work of

---

Box 9.1   Talking About Gaps

Here are a few examples of possible ways of announcing that there is a gap in the research literature which your study will help fill. Note the words and phrases that signal this rhetorical move—ones like "incomplete," "overlooked," and "rarely studied" as opposed to ones like "supplement," "enrich," and "another piece of the answer"—and how different choices create differences in tone. (To avoid appearing to criticize anyone, I have taken all these examples from my own work.)

I suggest that some of familiar ways of explaining why utterances and texts take the shapes they do result in incomplete explanations, because they take only the social into account and not the individual.

This article argues that self-expression is a crucial though heretofore largely overlooked part of the explanation for linguistic variation.

[This study] takes a perspective on sociolinguistic variation that supplements the results of studies of language use in relatively tight, focused, homogeneous communities.

In this chapter I want to show that attention to discourse-level aspects of regional variation can enrich the analysis of literary uses of dialect.

My first aim is to contribute to the empirical, descriptive study of the discursive practices of a group of female Americans who are rarely studied: white, middle-class, urban mid-westerners.

In this paper we report on a study designed to provide another piece of the answer to the question of whether women talk differently to women than they do to men, and if so, why.

others. Bear in mind that the mere fact that something has not been studied before is not itself a reason to study it (there are probably good reasons, for example, why there is such a dearth of research literature about the relationship between sociolinguistic variation and eye color): you have to show why it is important that your research space be filled in. You can also establish a research niche by raising new questions, or, conversely, by showing that you are continuing in an important research tradition.

One interesting way to elucidate your research niche is via a description of a scene encountered in an ethnographic study [Erikson (1986, pp. 149–150) calls this a "narrative vignette"] or a bit of text or transcript, accompanied by a series of questions that are raised by this snippet of data, or by a short, thought-provoking explanation that makes readers want to know more about it, or more about similar events or records. In a longer paper you might do both of these. The introduction then suggests how to fill the scholarly niche you have identified or refines the questions you have posed by suggesting what your specific research questions are and intimating (not yet detailing; that comes later) how you set about answering them. Sometimes, particularly in a longer paper, the structure of what follows is outlined: what happens where in the paper.

One effective introduction to an article is from a paper by Natalie Schilling-Estes (1998) called "Investigating 'self-conscious' speech: The performance register in Ocracoke English." Schilling-Estes' abstract begins with "this article examines;" the first sentence of the article switches to "I examine." (Regardless of what you may have been told in high school, first person pronouns are common and perfectly acceptable in scholarly writing.) Her initial sentence shows what her general territory is, performance speech, defines this concept, and suggests that Schilling-Estes' particular niche will involve articulating this concept with "mainstream language variationist" research in a way that has not been done before: "Here I examine a speech register that has received little attention in mainstream language variationist literature, namely PERFORMANCE SPEECH, defined as that register associated with speakers' attempting to display for others a certain language or language variety, whether their own or that of another speech community" (p. 53). Schilling-Estes then uses a discussion of the occasions on which performance speech occurs as a way to briefly review some of the treatments of it in the literature of dialect imitation, the ethnography of communication, and language obsolescence. Next, she again identifies the gap her work helps fill: "But despite the pervasiveness of performance speech, language variationists have tended to dismiss it, because their focus has traditionally been on unselfconscious or 'natural' speech" (pp. 53–54).

The second (and last) paragraph of Schilling-Estes' short introductory section begins with an announcement that her study is meant to fill the gap she has identified, and that doing so is important: "The current study shows that valuable insights about language variation can be gained through investigating performance speech" (p. 54). Then she states the specific claims for which she will argue in the paper: "In particular, I demonstrate that performance speech may display quite regular patterning. . . . Further, I show that patterns found in performance speech may help answer questions related to the perception of language features. . . . Finally, I argue that the incorporation of performance speech into language variation study offers evidence to support the growing belief that style-shifing may be primarily PROACTIVE rather than REACTIVE" (p. 54). The introduction ends with yet another niche-claiming move, as Schilling-Estes shows that this final claim is "in sharp contrast to traditional variationist-based views on style-shifting" (p. 54), which she very briefly sketches.

Literature Review. Whatever your introductory choices about how to engage the reader, it is necessary to put what you are doing in context. This invariably involves some sort of literature review, either integrated into the introduction or (sometimes less interestingly) as a separate labeled section. Here you describe other work that bears on your topic (not everything you have read—you do not get credit for pursuing the false leads, unfortunately—but everything that turned out to be relevant). Someone reading your paper should be able to trust it as a complete overview of your particular topic. A paper about whether shop employees talk differently to male than to female customers should, for example, describe all the work that has been done before on audience design correlated with gender in the context of service encounters. It would not be necessary, or necessarily even helpful, for such a paper to list all the work that has been done on language and gender in general, or on discourse in the workplace, although a few key references to each of these more inclusive areas would help demonstrate the author's familiarity with them. For example, the literature review section of an article by Kathleen Ferrara (1992) called "The interactive achievement of a sentence: Joint productions in therapeutic discourse" is labeled "Previous work on joint sentence productions." The literature review in a dissertation is of course more comprehensive, but even here it is important to show how the work you summarize contextualizes your particular argument. A series of book report-like treatments that just demonstrate that you have done the assigned or suggested reading would be more appropriate for an essay examination.

Methodology. Some research-paper formats require a section labeled "methods" or "methodology." Whether or not you call a section by one of these names, you need to describe how you did your work. This means being explicit about how you chose who or what to study, and why, about how you collected data, about how much data, or how many speakers, or how long you spent in the field, and about your analytical methods. It also means anticipating questions about representativeness and distribution: why didn't your sample include men, or African-Americans, for example, if it did not; in what ways are your results likely to be generalizable and in what ways are they unlikely to be? Bear in mind that the rhetorical function of this part of the paper is, in part, to show that you know what is important about the methodological decisions you made. (This means that you can undermine your own credibility if you include scientific-sounding but irrelevant details about methodology.) Schilling-Estes' article divides the discussion of her methodology into four sections. In "The sociolinguistic setting," she describes the community she studied and, briefly, the history and current status of the Ocracoke variety of English spoken there. "The rationale for a case-study format" not only describes an important aspect of her method but justifies it, in light of the fact that qualitative case studies contrast with the predominantly quantitative, large-scale studies in traditional research on variation. "Speaker characteristics" describes the person she studied and the recurrent phrase that was her focus, and "Acoustic data" describes the particular variable on which the quantitative part of her analysis was focused and the techniques she used in this analysis.

Findings. Obviously, the key element of a research paper is the description of results. If your research questions were well thought out in the first place (see Chapter 3), the organization of this part of the paper should be straightforward: you can simply answer each research question in turn. But in addition to suggesting answers to your research questions, an important function of this part of the paper is to make it clear what your evidence was for each answer, and that your evidence was sufficient. Whether your work is mainly ethnographic or mainly based on discourse analysis, assuring the reader that you have evidence for your claims requires moving back and forth between the particular and the general, between descriptions and analyses of particular scenes or texts and discussion of how often the patterns you find there occur in the larger corpus of scenes or texts you claim to be describing. You have to show that you are a sensitive and accurate noticer and interpreter of detail, and the way to do this is to demonstrate it with particular examples illustrating particular claims. You also have to show that you can move outward from your particular *explication de texte* or ethnographic vignette to well-founded suggestions about the workings of whatever interaction of language and society you are interested in.

One common difficulty in reporting the results of a research project is the temptation to let a narrative of the research process substitute for a retrospective analytical report about it: "First I did this, then I did that, then I discovered x, then I discovered y." Bear in mind that what you are describing is not what you *did*, but what you *found*. A chronological account of your activities may form part of your discussion of your methodology, but it is not the same as a research report.

Discussion.   One or more sections at the end of an article typically discuss the implications of the project's findings. Here writers comment, sometimes in a relatively speculative way, about what they have done. Often this involves summarizing, particularly if the paper is a long one. Sometimes it involves talking about what still needs to be done, or what the next step in the research will be. In every case it involves commenting on the significance of the project and the findings, highlighting—but not overstating—what is suggested by your findings that is important and new, what sociolinguists know now that we needed to know and did not know before. It is important to show that you are aware of what still needs to be done, but do not make too strong a case for the limitations of your project!

Box 9.2 Submitting Your Work

Whether submitting a term paper, an abstract for a conference presentation, or an article to a journal, there are some simple steps that can help make teachers, reviewers and editors more receptive.

- Illustrate the points you make with examples from your data. Put the examples in the body of the paper or article, not just in an appendix. Readers do not want to have to flip back and forth from text to appendix.
- Number the examples in the text, and refer to them by number (e.g., "As example 4 shows . . . ").
- Follow directions about length and format to the letter. If an abstract or a paper is too long, carelessly formatted, or formatted for some other journal or conference, it reflects badly on its author. For journal submissions, look at the journal's style sheet, which is usually inside the front or back cover of the journal. It will include instructions about citation format, spacing, margins, and so on, as well as instructions about how many copies to send and in what format(s). For conference abstracts, the directions (how long, how many copies, whether a separate reference list is acceptable) are usually part of the call for papers. For term papers, ask the instructor.
- Where you have choices about format (for example, if you can choose what font or type size to use), keep it simple, consistent, and traditional. Remember that what you are producing is a manuscript, not a finished publication, and that the traditional fonts and traditional conventions about spacing and margins are meant to make it easy for an editor to read and work on the manuscript. Even the cover page for a term paper should be simple and professional looking.
- Meet deadlines. Or submit things early.

Other Genres

The sort of research article described in the preceding section is modeled on (and has evolved historically from) research reports in science and quantitative social science. The format of such an article makes it relatively easy to include general statements and relatively difficult to include longer examples of discourse or to take readers through close analyses of them. It is almost impossible in this format to let readers hear the voices you studied. (In my own experience, anonymous reviewers' responses to drafts in the traditional research-article format almost always call for more generality—more theoretical background and more general speculation about implications—without more length, which means that examples and line-by-line analyses have to be shortened or removed.) Erikson (1986, p. 145) suggests that the readers of qualitative research reports should function as "coanalysts," but the research article makes it difficult to encourage this.

Another model for reporting the results of interpretive research comes from the humanities rather than the sciences. This is the essay. Many sociolinguists have some familiarity with the literary-critical essay, in which the reader is slowly guided from a particular observation—a line of a poem, a description of a character in a play, a synopsis of part of a plot—to a general suggestion about how a particular work can be read, or about reading in general. Essays are not the preferred format in sociolinguistics, and our journals rarely publish research reports in essay format (there are articles, not essays, in *Language in Society,* for example), so anyone who needs the standard kinds of scholarly credits toward employability or tenure needs to be able to write articles. But there are venues for essays, too: edited volumes, single-authored collections, journals in neighboring fields such as rhetoric and critical theory, or the Internet.

A. L. Becker (1995, p. 431) uses Clifford Geertz' (1980) distinction between "laws-and-instances" and "cases-and-interpretations" modes of explanation to describe the difference between articles and essays. In the former, the argument starts with a research question that situates the researcher in a particular gap in previous work, and data are used to propose answers to the question. In the latter, we start with some language and, to use Becker's metaphor, "translate" it, unpack it, show how a systematic asking of questions, aided by the sorts of heuristics we have talked about above, can help us see exactly why the data are the way they are and no other way. An essay is "an informed exploration of a particular text" (Becker, 1994, p. 163) whose rigor comes from the care and systematicity with which it is done. Only after exploring a particular text in detail does an essayist make more general suggestions about how such texts or such situations or such ways of talking might usually or always work. Spradley (1980, p. 162) talks about ethnographic writing as translation, too. What Spradley says about ethnography is true for talking about qualitative work in general: "In writing an ethnography, as translation in the full sense, *the concern for the general is incidental to an understanding of the particular.*"

There are other possibilities, too. Qualitative researchers in other fields have experimented, for example, with autobiographical writing as a way to capture the process of interpretation on which qualitative research is based. [Many of the chapters in Josselson (1996) are narratives of this sort.] Particularly in live situations such as conferences, multimedia presentations that include performances are possible—there are ways, in other words, to "show" your findings rather than simply telling about them. Sociolinguists have, of course, long thought of the playing of taped examples as a key part of the presentation of our results. Visual images are becoming more common in printed media, now that the technology for digitizing, transmitting, and printing pictures has begun to make this more feasible than it once was. Electronic publishing provides new options, too, for the inclusion of film with text, for example; this medium seems likely to become more and more legitimate as a venue for sociolinguists' research reports. And, of course, sociolinguists have the responsibility for making our findings accessible to people in the wider world, which means presenting our work in textbooks, lectures, and interviews, among other things.

The Grammar of Particularity

Whether writing an article or an essay, there are simple grammatical ways of making sure you are not claiming more than you mean to claim and of encouraging readers to hear the voices of the people you studied. For one thing, you can think carefully about how to refer to your research subjects. It has become so common in the social sciences to use (pseudonymous) first names for reference to research

subjects that we have almost stopped noticing how this can deper-
sonalize people. If you are really on a first-name basis with the people you study, then using first names to refer to them may help recre-
ate the situation and the social relations. But if you did not call them
by their first names, or would not if you knew them, or if they might
not want to be referred to with first names, then think about using
pseudonymous last names, with appropriate titles, instead.

Another way to help ensure that your particular descriptions stay
particular is to use the past tense rather than the present tense in descriptions of people's actions or words. Think about the difference
between the (a) versions and the (b) versions in these examples:

(9.1a) Mrs. Blair uses nonstandard forms rarely.
(9.1b) Mrs. Blair used nonstandard forms rarely.

(9.2a) In casual conversation, women are interrupted more
        than men.
(9.2b) In casual conversation, women were interrupted more
        than men.

As you can see, the present-tense versions make subtle claims to
generality that the past-tense versions do not. And the narrative
past tense helps keep reminding readers (and ourselves) that we are
talking about a particular study, which took place in a particular
place and time. It has become customary in linguistics to talk about
decontextualized texts in the present tense, talking, for example,
about what "happens in line 16" rather than what a speaker said or
a writer wrote at some particular point in time, and although this
convention can be useful it should not be used unthinkingly.

A related effect comes from making sure you refer to the situations and people you studied in definite ways: "these women," not
"women"; "in this conversation" rather than "in conversation."
Thus an even better version of sentence (9.2) above might be (9.2c):

(9.2c) In the casual conversations I recorded, the women were
        interrupted more than the men.

Doing this helps ensure that you do not make the leap to generality
(all women are always interrupted more than men) unintentionally

or prematurely—or dishonestly—and that when you do extrapolate from your study, readers know exactly what your evidence is.

Summary

This chapter discussed two of the most common genres in which sociolinguists write: the article and the essay. We also touched on some ways to ensure that you are not making implicit generalizations that are not warranted by your analysis. There are many other facets of academic writing that could have been dealt with here: how to summarize research studies, for example, or where the line is between making the case for the importance of your work and overstating it. The best way to learn to write, though, is probably by reading, and while sociolinguistics has its share of awkward writers, the field's major journals and books include many very good examples of these and other genres.

This book has probably raised more questions about research methods in readers' minds than it has answered. This is inevitable and intentional. Thinking about method is something we do anew every time we plan a new project. Very few sociolinguists choose one approach and use it over and over. At the very least, we vary our methods as our research questions become more focused and more sophisticated. Sometimes, new questions, new technologies, and new research sites call for completely new methods: new sources of data, new ways of collecting them, new modes of analysis, and new modes of writing. The trick is not to learn the correct way to work, but to be able to think carefully in each new situation about the best way to work.

It is also important to remember that no set of methods is perfect or works perfectly. It is conventional to talk or write about research, after the fact, in a way that suggests that every detail was planned in advance, every glitch anticipated, and every step followed exactly as described, and that everything worked exactly as foreseen. In fact, this happens rarely, if ever. We are always revising, subtracting and adding, wishing we had done some things differently from the beginning, coping with new problems and taking advantage of new opportunities as our research progresses. The best any of us do is to think very carefully about our plans before we start and document exactly what we do as we progress.

DISCUSSION QUESTIONS

1. Choose an issue of *Language in Society* or the *Journal of Sociolinguistics* and read one article in it on a topic that interests you. Then prepare a class presentation in which you talk about whether, and if so where in the article, the elements discussed above can be found (abstract, introduction, methodology, and so on). Are there any other elements? Are sections labeled? If so, do you find this useful? What do you think of the article's title? Has the author made any syntactic choices in the article that create unwarranted generalizations?

2. Study the abstracts of several articles in one or more of the same journals, and see if you can come up with a general rule about what article abstracts consist of. If you are writing a term paper for the course, write an abstract for it.

3. Write a short essay about the text you analyzed for Discussion Question 4 in Chapter 8 or the speech event you described for Discussion Question 2 in Chapter 7. Start with your text or speech event and your analysis, then work outward to more general questions it raises. If you do the speech event, you might start with what Erikson (1986, p. 151) calls an "ethnographic vignette," a narrative about the event told from the perspective of an insider. Or you might start by describing the event from an outsider's perspective, then raise questions about the meaning of your observations.

SUGGESTIONS FOR FURTHER READING

Swales (1990) reviews the literature about genres of academic writing, of which the article is one, and adds interesting findings of his own. The most reliable sources of examples of research articles in qualitative sociolinguistics are the field's major journals, because the peer review process tends to encourage thoroughness in what is included and discourage creativity in how it is presented. Chapters in many edited volumes are more mixed in genre, combining aspects of essay and article style. Wonderful examples of essays are in Becker (1995). Books dealing with writing about qualitative research in general (not just in sociolinguistics) are Wolcott (1990), Denzin (1996), and Ely et al. (1997).

References

Agar, M. H. (1996a). *Schon wieder?* Science in linguistic anthropology. *Anthropology Newsletter*, 37(1), 13.

Agar, M. H. (1996b). *The professional stranger: An informal introduction to ethnography* (2nd ed.). San Diego: Academic Press.

Alasuutari, P. (1995). *Researching culture: Qualitative method and cultural studies*. Beverly Hills: Sage.

Allen, H. B. (1956). The linguistic atlases: Our new resource. *The English Journal*, 45, 188–194.

Allen, H. B. (1973–1976). *The linguistic atlas of the upper midwest* (Vols. 1–3). Minneapolis: University of Minnesota Press.

Allen, H. B. and Underwood, G. N. (Eds.). (1971). *Readings in American dialectology*. New York: Appleton-Century-Crofts.

Altheide, D. L. and Johnson, J. M. (1994). Criteria for assessing interpretive validity in qualitative research. In N. K. Denzin and Y. S. Lincoln (Eds.), *Handbook of qualitative research* (pp. 485–499). Thousand Oaks, CA: Sage.

Atwood, E. B. (1971). The methods of American dialectology. In H. B. Allen and G. Underwood (Eds.), *Readings in American dialectology* (pp. 5–35). New York: Appleton-Century-Crofts. [Originally published in 1963 in *Zeitschrift für Mundartforschung*, 30(1), 1–29.]

Bailey, G. (1991). Directions of change in Texas English. *Journal of American Culture*, 14, 125–134.

Bailey, G. (1993). A perspective on African-American English. In D. R. Preston (Ed.), *American dialect research* (pp. 287–318). Amsterdam: John Benjamins.

Baugh, J. (1993). Adapting dialectology: The conduct of community language studies. In D. R. Preston (Ed.), *American dialect research* (pp. 167–191). Amsterdam: John Benjamins.

Bauman, R. (1977). *Verbal art as performance*. Rowley, MA: Newbury House. Reprinted 1984, Prospect Heights, IL: Waveland Press.

Bauman, R. and Sherzer, J. (Eds.). (1974). *Explorations in the ethnography of speaking*. Cambridge: Cambridge University Press.

Bauman, R. and Sherzer, J. (Eds.). (1989). *Explorations in the ethnography of speaking* (2nd ed.). Cambridge: Cambridge University Press.

Bean, J. M. and Johnstone, B. (1994). Workplace reasons for saying you're sorry: Discourse management and apology in telephone interviews. *Discourse Processes, 17*, 59–81.

Becker, A. L. (1975). A linguistic image of nature: The Burmese numerative classifier system. *International Journal of the Sociology of Language, 5*, 109–121.

Becker, A. L. (1988). Language in particular: A lecture. In D. Tannen (Ed.), *Linguistics in context: Connecting observation and understanding* (pp. 17–35). Norwood, NJ: Ablex.

Becker, A. L. (1994). Repetition and otherness: An essay. In B. Johnstone (Ed.), *Repetition in discourse: Interdisciplinary perspectives* (Vol. II, pp. 162–175). Norwood, NJ: Ablex.

Becker, A. L. (1995). *Beyond translation: Essays toward a modern philology*. Ann Arbor: University of Michigan Press.

Biber, D. (1988). *Variation across speech and writing*. Cambridge: Cambridge University Press.

Biber, D. and Finegan, E. (1989). Styles of stance in English: Lexical and grammatical marking of evidentiality and affect. *Text, 9*, 93–124.

Bing, J. and Bergvall, V. (Eds.). (1996). *Rethinking language and gender research: Theory and practice*. New York: Longman.

Bloomfield, L. (1933). *Language*. New York: Holt.

Bloomfield, L. (1948). *Outline guide for the practical study of foreign languages*. Baltimore: Linguistic Society of America.

Bouquiaux, L. and Thomas, J. M. C. (1992). *Studying and describing unwritten languages*. (J. Roberts, trans.). Dallas, TX: Summer Institute of Linguistics. (Original work published in 1976.)

Briggs, C. L. (1986). *Learning how to ask: A sociolinguistic appraisal of the role of the interview in social science research*. Cambridge: Cambridge University Press.

Brown, G. and Yule, G. (1983). *Discourse analysis*. Cambridge: Cambridge University Press.

Brown, P. and Levinson, S. C. (1987). *Politeness: Some universals in language usage*. Cambridge: Cambridge University Press.

Bucholtz, M. (1997). *Borrowed Blackness: African American vernacular English and European American youth identities*. Unpublished doctoral dissertation, University of California at Berkeley.

Cameron, D. (1992). 'Respect, Please!': Investigating race, power, and language. In D. Cameron, E. Frazer, P. Harvey, M. B. H. Rampton, and K. Richardson (Eds.), *Researching language: Issues of power and method* (pp. 113–130). London: Routledge.

Cameron, D., Frazer, E., Harvey, P., Rampton, M. B. H., and Richardson, K. (Eds.). (1992). *Researching language: Issues of power and method*. London: Routledge.

Cassidy, F. G. (Ed.). (1985, 1991, 1996). *Dictionary of American regional English*. Cambridge, MA: Harvard University Press.

Cassidy, F. G. (1993). Area lexicon: The making of DARE. In D. R. Preston (Ed.), *American dialect research* (pp. 93–105). Amsterdam: John Benjamins.

Chafe, W. (Ed.). (1980). *The Pear stories: Cognitive, cultural, and linguistic aspects of narrative production*. Norwood, NJ: Ablex.

Chafe, W. (1994). *Discourse, consciousness, and time*. Chicago: University of Chicago Press.

Chambers, J. K. and Trudgill, P. (1980). *Dialectology*. Cambridge: Cambridge University Press.

Chandler, J., Davidson, A. I., and Harootunian, H. (Eds.). (1994). *Questions of evidence: Proof, practice, and persuasion across the disciplines*. Chicago: University of Chicago Press.

Cloarec-Heiss, F. (1992). Questionnaire 6: Verb phrase. In L. Bouquiaux and J. M. C. Thomas (Eds.), *Studying and describing unwritten languages.* (J. Roberts, trans.) (pp. 257–270.) Dallas, TX: Summer Institute of Linguistics.

Coates, J. (1996). *Women talk: Conversation between women friends.* Oxford: Blackwell.

Cresswell, J. (1994). *Research design: Qualitative and quantitative approaches.* Thousand Oaks, CA: Sage.

Cukor-Avila, P. (1996, March). *The long and the short of it: The importance of longitudinal studies in sociolinguistic research.* Paper presented at Southeastern Conference on Linguistics, College Station, TX.

Cushing, S. (1994). *Fatal words: Communication clashes and aircraft crashes.* Chicago: University of Chicago Press.

Denzin, N. K. (1996). *Interpretive ethnography: Ethnographic practices for the 21st century.* Thousand Oaks, CA: Sage.

Denzin, N. K. and Lincoln, Y. S. (Eds.). (1994). *Handbook of qualitative research.* Beverly Hills, CA: Sage.

Dorval, B. (Ed.). (1990). *Conversational organization and its development.* Norwood, NJ: Ablex.

Eckert, P. and McConnell-Ginet, S. (1992). Think practically and look locally: Language and gender as community-based practice. *Annual Review of Anthropology, 21,* 461–490.

Edwards, J. A. and Lampert, M. D. (Eds.). (1993). *Talking data: Transcription and coding in discourse research.* Hillsdale, NJ: Lawrence Erlbaum.

Ely, M., Vinz, R., Downing, M., and Anzul, M. (1997). *On writing qualitative research: Living by words.* London: Falmer Press.

Emerson, R. M. (1995). *Writing ethnographic fieldnotes.* Chicago: University of Chicago Press.

Erikson, F. (1986). Qualitative methods in research on teaching. In M. C. Wittock (Ed.), *Handbook of research on teaching* (pp. 119–161). New York: Macmillan.

Fairclough, N. L. (1985). Critical and descriptive goals in discourse analysis. *Journal of Pragmatics, 9,* 739–763.

Fasold, R. (1984). *The sociolinguistics of society.* Oxford: Basil Blackwell.

Fasold, R. (1990). *The sociolinguistics of language.* Oxford: Basil Blackwell.

Ferrara, K. (1992). The interactive achievement of a sentence: Joint productions in therapeutic discourse. *Discourse Processes, 15,* 207–228.

Ferrara, K. (1994). *Therapeutic ways with words.* Oxford: Oxford University Press.

Finch, J. (1984). It's great to have someone to talk to—the ethics and politics of interviewing women. In C. Bell and H. Roberts (Eds.), *Social researching* (pp. 70–87). London: Routledge and Kegan Paul.

Flower, L., Stein, V., Ackerman, J., Kantz, M. J., McCormick, K., and Peck, W. C. (1990). *Reading to write: Exploring a cognitive and social process.* New York: Oxford University Press.

Foucault, M. (1980). *Power/Knowledge: Selected interviews and other writings, 1972–1977.* C. Gordon (Ed.). New York: Pantheon.

Francis, W. N. (1993). The historical and cultural interpretation of dialect. In D. R. Preston (Ed.), *American dialect research* (pp. 13–30). Amsterdam: John Benjamins.

Friedrich, P. (1986). *The language parallax.* Austin: University of Texas Press.

Geertz, C. (1980). Blurred genres: The refiguration of social thought. *The American Scholar, 49*(2).

Geertz, C. (1983). *Local knowledge: Further essays in interpretive anthropology.* New York: Basic Books.

Glaser, B. and Strauss, A. (1967). *The discovery of grounded theory.* Chicago: Aldine.

Goffman, E. (1974). *Frame analysis.* New York: Harper & Row.

Gumperz, J. J. (1982). *Discourse strategies.* Cambridge: Cambridge University Press.

Gumperz, J. J. and Hymes, D. (Eds.). (1972). *Directions in sociolinguistics: Ethnography of communication.* New York: Holt, Rinehart & Winston.

Hamilton, H. E. (1994). *Conversations with an Alzheimer's patient.* Cambridge: Cambridge University Press.

Hammersley, M. and Atkinson, P. (1983). *Ethnography: Principles in practice.* London: Tavistock Publications.

Harris, Z. S. (1951). *Structural linguistics.* Chicago: University of Chicago Press.

Harvey, P. (1992). Bilingualism in the Peruvian Andes. In D. Cameron, E. Frazer, P. Harvey, M. B. H. Rampton, and K. Richardson (Eds.), *Researching language: Issues of power and method* (pp. 65–89). London: Routledge.

Heath, S. B. (1983). *Ways with words: Language, life, and work in communities and classrooms*. Cambridge: Cambridge University Press.

Hodge, R. and Kress, G. (1993). *Language as ideology* (2nd ed.). New York: Routledge.

Hudson, R. A. (1996). *Sociolinguistics* (2nd ed). Cambridge: Cambridge University Press.

Hurston, Z. N. (1937). *Their eyes were watching God*. Urbana: University of Illinois Press.

Hymes, D. (1972). Models of the interaction of language and social life. In J. J. Gumperz and D. Hymes (Eds.), *Directions in sociolinguistics: Ethnography of communication* (pp. 35–71). New York: Holt, Rinehart & Winston.

Hymes, D. (1974). *Foundations in sociolinguistics: An ethnographic approach*. Philadelphia: University of Pennsylvania Press.

Hymes, D. (1978). *What is ethnography?* (Sociolinguistics Working Paper #45.) Austin, TX: Southwest Educational Development Laboratory.

Jeffers, R. J. and Lehiste, I. (1979). *Principles and methods for historical linguistics*. Cambridge, MA: MIT Press.

Johnson, E. (1996). *Lexical change and variation in the southeastern United States, 1930–1990*. Tuscaloosa: University of Alabama Press.

Johnstone, A. C. (1994). *Uses for journal-keeping: An ethnography of writing in a university science class*. Norwood, NJ: Ablex.

Johnstone, B. (1990). *Stories, community, and place: Narratives from middle America*. Bloomington: Indiana University Press.

Johnstone, B. (1996). *The linguistic individual: Self-expression in language and linguistics*. New York: Cambridge University Press.

Johnstone, B. and Bean, J. M. (1997). Self-expression and linguistic variation. *Language in Society, 26*, 221–246.

Johnstone, B., Ferrara, K., and Bean, J. M. (1992). Gender, politeness, and discourse management in same-sex and cross-sex opinion-poll interviews. *Journal of Pragmatics, 18*, 405–430.

Jorgensen, D. L. (1989). *Participant observation: A methodology for human studies*. Newbury Park, CA: Sage.

Josselson, R. (Ed.). (1996). *Ethics and process in the narrative study of lives*. Thousand Oaks, CA: Sage.

Kibrik, A. E. (1977). *The methodology of field investigations in linguistics: Setting up the problem*. The Hague: Mouton.

Kiesling, S. F. (1997). Power and the language of men. In S. Johnson and U. H. Meinhof (Eds.), *Language and masculinity* (pp. 65–85). Oxford: Blackwell.

Killingsworth, M. J. (1996). Discourse community. In T. Enos (Ed.), *Encyclopedia of rhetoric and composition* (pp. 194–196). New York: Garland.

Killingsworth, M. J. and Palmer, J. S. (1992). *Ecospeak: Rhetoric and environmental politics in America*. Carbondale: Southern Illinois University Press.

Kirk, J. and Miller, M. L. (1986). *Reliability and validity in qualitative research*. Beverly Hills, CA: Sage.

Kretzschmar, W. A., Jr. et al. (1993). *Handbook of the linguistic atlas of the middle and south atlantic states*. Chicago: University of Chicago Press.

Kurath, H. et al. (1939–43). *The linguistic atlas of New England* (Vols. 1–3). Providence: Brown University, for the American Council of Learned Societies. (Reprinted 1972, New York: AMS.)

Labov, W. (1966). *The social stratification of English in New York City*. Washington, DC: Center for Applied Linguistics.

Labov, W. (1972a). Some principles of linguistic methodology. *Language in Society*, *1*, 97–120.

Labov, W. (1972b). *Sociolinguistic patterns*. Philadelphia: University of Pennsylvania Press.

Labov, W. (1972c). The linguistic consequences of being a lame. In W. Labov, *Language in the inner city* (pp. 255–292). Philadelphia: University of Pennsylvania Press.

Labov, W. (1982). Objectivity and commitment in linguistic science: The case of the Black English trial in Ann Arbor. *Language in Society*, *11*, 165–201.

Labov, W. (1984). Field methods of the project on linguistic change and variation. In J. Baugh and J. Sherzer (Eds.), *Language in use: Readings in sociolinguistics* (pp. 28–66). Englewood Cliffs, NJ: Prentice-Hall.

Lakoff, R. (1975). *Language and woman's place*. New York: Harper & Row.

Larmouth, D. W. (1992). The legal and ethical status of surreptitious recording in dialect research: Do human subjects guidelines apply? In *Legal and ethical issues in surreptitious recording* (Publication of the American Dialect Society, #76, pp. 1–14). Tuscaloosa: The University of Alabama Press, for the American Dialect Society.

Lindlof, T. R. (1995). *Qualitative communication research methods*. Beverly Hills, CA: Sage.

Lindquist, J. L. (1995). *"Bullshit on 'what if' ": An ethnographic rhetoric of political argument in a working-class bar*. Unpublished doctoral dissertation, University of Illinois at Chicago.

Luebs, M. (1996). *Frozen speech: The rhetoric of transcription*. Unpublished doctoral dissertation, University of Michigan.

Macaulay, R. K. S. (1991). *Locating dialect in discourse: The language of honest men and bonnie lasses in Ayr*. New York: Oxford University Press.

McDavid, R. I., Jr. (1976–1978). *The linguistic atlas of the North-Central states: Basic materials*. (Chicago microfilm manuscripts on cultural anthropology, N. McQuown, Ed., series 38.200–208.) Chicago: Joseph Regenstein Library, University of Chicago.

McLemore, C. A. (1991). *The pragmatic interpretation of English intonation: Sorority speech*. Unpublished doctoral dissertation, University of Texas at Austin.

McLeod-Porter, D. (1991). *Gender, ethnicity, and narrative: A linguistic and rhetorical analysis of adolescents' personal experience stories*. Unpublished doctoral dissertation, Texas A&M University.

Merritt, M. (1977). The playback: An instance of variation in discourse. In R. W. Fasold and R. W. Shuy (Eds.), *Studies in language variation: Semantics, syntax, phonology, pragmatics, social situations, ethnographic approaches* (proceedings of the Colloquium on New Ways of Analyzing Variation, 3rd, Georgetown University, 1974, pp. 198– 208). Washington, DC: Georgetown University Press.

Milroy, L. (1987a). *Observing and analyzing natural language: A critical account of sociolinguistic method*. Oxford: Basil Blackwell.

Milroy, L. (1987b). *Language and social networks* (2nd ed.). Oxford: Basil Blackwell.

Mukherjee, D. (1995). *Ethnic identity and language use by women in the immigrant Malaysian–Bengali community.* Unpublished doctoral dissertation, Texas A&M University.

Murray, T. E. and Murray, C. R. (1992). On the legality and ethics of surreptitious recording. In *Legal and ethical issues in surreptitious recording* (Publication of the American Dialect Society, #76, pp. 15–75). Tuscaloosa: The University of Alabama Press, for the American Dialect Society.

Murray, T. E., with the assistance of Murray, C. D. R. (1996). *Under cover of law: More on the legality of surreptitious recording* (Publication of the American Dialect Society, #79). Tuscaloosa: The University of Alabama Press, for the American Dialect Society.

Nelson, J. S., Megill, A., and McCloskey, D. N. (Eds.). (1987). *The rhetoric of the human sciences: Language and argument in scholarship and public affairs.* Madison: University of Wisconsin Press.

Newman, P. (1992). Fieldwork and field methods in linguistics. *California Linguistic Notes, 23,* 1, 3–8.

Oakley, A. (1981). Interviewing women. In H. Roberts (Ed.), *Doing feminist research.* London: Routledge and Kegan Paul.

O'Barr, W. and Atkins, B. K. (1980). "Women's language" or "powerless language"? In S. McConnell-Ginet, R. Borker, and N. Furman (Eds.), *Women and language in literature and society* (pp. 93–110). New York: Praeger.

Ochs, E. (1979). Transcription as theory. In E. Ochs and B. B. Schieffelin (Eds.), *Developmental pragmatics* (pp. 43–72). New York: Academic Press.

O'Connor, P. (1995). Speaking of crime: "I don't know what made me do it." *Discourse & Society, 6,* 429–456.

Paulston, C. B. and Tucker, G. R. (Eds.). (1997). *The early days of sociolinguistics: Memories and reflections.* Dallas, TX: Summer Institute of Linguistics.

Pederson, L. (1974). Tape/text and analogues. *American Speech, 49,* 5–23.

Pederson, L. (1993). An approach to linguistic geography. In D. R. Preston (Ed.), *American dialect research* (pp. 31–92). Amsterdam: John Benjamins.

Pederson, L., McDaniel, S. L., and Dent, B. D. (1986–1992). *Linguistic atlas of the Gulf states* (Vols. 1–7). Athens: University of Georgia Press.

Pera, M. (1994). *The discourses of science.* Chicago: The University of Chicago Press.

Polanyi, L. (1985). *Telling the American story: A structural and cultural analysis of conversational storytelling.* Norwood, NJ: Ablex.

Pratt, M. L. (1977). *Toward a speech act theory of literary discourse.* Bloomington: Indiana University Press.

Pratt, M. L. (1987). Linguistic utopias. In N. Fabb, D. Attridge, A. Durant, and C. MacCabe (Eds.), *The linguistics of writing: Arguments between language and literature* (pp. 48–66). New York: Methuen.

Preston, D. R. (1985). The Li'l Abner syndrome: Written representations of speech. *American Speech, 60,* 328–337.

Radford, A. (1988). *Transformational grammar: A first course.* Cambridge: Cambridge University Press.

Rakow, L. (1992). *Gender on the line: Women, the telephone, and community life.* Urbana: University of Illinois Press.

Rampton, B. (1995a.) Politics and change in research in applied linguistics. *Applied Linguistics, 16,* 233–256.

Rampton, B. (1995b.) *Crossing: Language and ethnicity among adolescents.* London: Longman

Rampton, M. B. H. (1992). Scope for empowerment in sociolinguistics? In D. Cameron, E. Frazer, P. Harvey, M. B. H. Rampton, and K. Richardson (Eds.), *Researching language: Issues of power and method* (pp. 29–64). London: Routledge.

Renkema, J. (1993). *Discourse studies: An introductory textbook.* Philadelphia: John Benjamins.

Ross, J. R. (1979). Where's English? In C. J. Fillmore, D. Kempler, and W. S.-Y. Wang (Eds.), *Individual differences in language ability and language behavior* (pp. 127–163). New York: Academic Press.

Samarin, W. J. (1967). *Field linguistics: A guide to linguistic field work.* New York: Holt, Rinehart & Winston.

Saville-Troike, M. (1989). *The ethnography of communication: An introduction* (2nd ed.). Cambridge, MA: Blackwell.

Schiffrin, D. (1984). How a story says what it means and does. *Text*, 4, 13–346.

Schiffrin, D. (1987). *Discourse markers*. Cambridge: Cambridge University Press.

Schiffrin, D. (1994). *Approaches to discourse*. Oxford: Blackwell.

Schilling-Estes, N. (1998). Investigating "self-conscious" speech: The performance register in Ocracoke English. *Language in Society, 27*, 53–83.

Schnebly, C. (1994). Repetition and failed conversation in the Theater of the Absurd. In B. Johnstone (Ed.), *Repetition in discourse* (Vol. II, pp. 98–112). Norwood, NJ: Ablex.

Sherzer, J. (1983). *Kuna ways of speaking: An ethnographic perspective*. Austin: University of Texas Press.

Shultz, J. J. and Erickson, F. (1982). *The counselor as gatekeeper: Social action in interviews*. New York: Academic Press.

Shuy, R. W. (1986). Ethical issues in analyzing FBI surreptitious tapes. *International Journal of the Sociology of Language, 62*, 119–128.

Spradley, J. P. (1979). *The ethnographic interview*. New York: Holt, Rinehart & Winston.

Spradley, J. P. (1980). *Participant observation*. New York: Holt, Rinehart & Winston.

Stocking, G. W., Jr. (1983). History of anthropology: Whence/whither. In G. W. Stocking, Jr. (Ed.), *Observers observed: Essays on ethnographic fieldwork* (pp. 3–11). Madison: University of Wisconsin Press.

Strauss, A. and Schatzman, L. (1955). Cross-class interviewing: An analysis of interaction and communicative styles. *Human Organization, 14*(2), 28–31.

Stubbs, M. (1983). *Discourse analysis: The sociolinguistic analysis of natural language*. Chicago: The University of Chicago Press.

Stubbs, M. (1996). *Text and corpus analysis: Computer-assisted studies of language and culture*. Oxford: Blackwell.

Swales, J. M. (1990). *Genre analysis: English in academic and research settings*. Cambridge: Cambridge University Press.

Tannen, D. (1979). What's in a frame? Surface evidence for underlying expectations. In R. Freedle (Ed.), *New directions in discourse processing* (pp. 137–181). Norwood, NJ: Ablex. Reprinted in D. Tannen (Ed.), *Framing in discourse* (pp. 14–56). New York: Oxford University Press.

Tannen, D. (1981). New York Jewish conversational style. *International Journal of the Sociology of Language*, 30, 133–149.

Tannen, D. (1982). Oral and literate strategies in spoken and written narratives. *Language*, 58, 1–21.

Tannen, D. (1984). *Conversational style: Analyzing talk among friends*. Norwood, NJ: Ablex.

Tannen, D. (1994). *Gender & discourse*. New York: Oxford University Press.

Tedlock, D. (1983). *The spoken word and the work of interpretation*. Philadelphia: University of Pennsylvania Press.

Trudgill, P. (1972). Sex and covert prestige: Linguistic change in the urban dialect of Norwich. *Language in Society*, 1, 179–195.

Urciuoli, B. (1995). Language and borders. *Annual Review of Anthropology*, 24, 525–546.

van Dijk, T. (Ed.). (1997). *Discourse studies: A multidisciplinary introduction* (Vols. 1 and 2). Thousand Oaks, CA: Sage.

van Maanen, J. (1995). *Representation in ethnography*. Thousand Oaks, CA: Sage.

Verscheuren, J., Östman, J.-A., and Blommaert, J. (Eds.). (1995). *Handbook of pragmatics: The manual*. Amsterdam: John Benjamins.

Wardhaugh, R. (1997). *An introduction to sociolinguistics* (3rd ed). Cambridge, MA: Blackwell.

Westcott, M. R. (1994). Intuition. In R. J. Corsini (Ed.), *Encyclopedia of psychology* (Vol. 2, pp. 288–291). New York: John Wiley.

Whorf, B. L. (1941). The relation of habitual thought and behavior to language. In L. Spier (Ed.), *Language, culture, and personality: Essays in memory of Edward Sapir* (pp. 75–93). Mehasha, WI: Sapir Memorial Publication Fund. Reprinted in J. B. Carroll (Ed.), *Language, thought, and reality: Selected writings of Benjamin Lee Whorf* (pp. 134–159). Cambridge, MA: MIT Press and New York: John Wiley.

Wild, K. W. (1983). *Intuition*. Cambridge: Cambridge University Press.

Wolcott, H. F. (1990). *Writing up qualitative research*. Thousand Oaks, CA: Sage.

Wolfson, N. (1976). Speech events and natural speech: Some implications for sociolinguistic methodology. *Language in Society, 5,* 188–209.

Young, R. E., Becker, A. L., and Pike, K. L. (1970). *Rhetoric: Discovery and change.* New York: Harcourt, Brace, and World.

Zimmerman, D. H. and West, C. (1975). Sex roles, interruptions and silences in conversation. In B. Thorne and N. Henley (Eds.), *Language and sex: Difference and dominance* (pp. 105–129). Rowley, MA: Newbury House.

Index